Haydn R
Junior Er
Revised ~~Edition~~

Revised by Angela Burt
Adviser: Patricia Lewis

GINN

Acknowledgements

Grateful acknowlegement is made to the following for permission to use copyright material:

page 6–7 **Attacked by a crow**
Watership Down by Richard Adams, published by Penguin Books. By kind permission of David Higham Associates Ltd.

12–13 **Toad and company**
The Wind in the Willows by Kenneth Grahame, copyright under the Berne Convention, reproduced by kind permission of Curtis Brown, London.

24 **Rikki-tikki and Darzee**
The Jungle Book by Rudyard Kipling. By kind permission of A P Watt Ltd on behalf of The National Trust for Places of Historical Interest or Natural Beauty.

30 **William's Workshop**
William's Workshop by Susan Gates, published by Ginn and Company. By kind permission of David Higham Associates Ltd.

48–49 **Inside the vault**
The Ghost of Thomas Kempe by Penelope Lively, published by William Heinemann Ltd. By kind permission of Reed Consumer Books Ltd.

54 **A pony for Jody**
The Red Pony by John Steinbeck, published by William Heinemann Ltd. By kind permission of Reed Consumer Books Ltd.

66 **Tarka fights Deadlock**
Tarka the Otter by Henry Williams, published by The Bodley Head Ltd. By kind permission of Randon House UK Ltd.

78 **Johann Gutenberg**
Twenty Inventors by Jacqueline Dineen, published by Wayland Publishers Ltd. By kind permission of Wayland Publishers Ltd.

84 **A fight in a signal-tower**
The Eagle of the Ninth by Rosemary Sutcliff, published by Oxford University Press. By kind permission of Oxford University Press.

Every effort has been made to obtain permission to use copyright materials. The publishers would be grateful for any discrepancies to be notified.

Designed by Michael Soderberg
Illustrated by Barry Rowe, Martin White, Beverly Curl, David Atkinson, Caroline Bilson, Vali Herzer and Hardlines.

© Haydn Richards 1965
Revised edition 1997
Second impression 2006
ISBN 0 602 27541 8 / 978 0602 275419 (without answers)
ISBN 0 602 22551 5 / 978 0602 225513 (with answers)

Published by Ginn and Company
Prebendal House, Parson's Fee
Aylesbury, Bucks HP20 2QY
Ginn on the Internet http://www.ginn.co.uk
Filmset by Wyvern Typesetting Ltd, Bristol
Printed in Great Britain by Ashford Colour Press Ltd.

Preface to the Revised Edition

This revised and updated edition of Haydn Richards' popular series meets the appropriate requirements of the 1995 National Curriculum for English at Key Stage 1 and Key Stage 2. It is also in line with the requirements of the Northern Ireland and Scottish 5-14 curricula.

Particular care has been taken while incorporating changes to preserve the successful format, tone and clarity of the original series.

Those already familiar with Junior English will see that in this revised edition there is now increased coverage of spelling, punctuation and grammar topics in each of the four books and that formal grammatical terminology, in response to popular request, is now used from the very beginning. Throughout the series, both the range and complexity of the reading comprehension exercises have been extended. Additional vocabulary exercises have been introduced together with a number of dictionary practice exercises to encourage the early use of dictionaries and thesauruses.

The series, as well as preparing pupils for National Curriculum assessment, also provides a sound basis for those preparing for 11+ English entrance examinations to independent schools. The current ISEB 11+ English syllabus was taken into account during the revision of Junior English.

Angela Burt

Contents

Nouns

The **butcher** gave the **dog** a big meaty **bone**.

Butcher is the name of a **person**.
Dog is the name of an **animal**.
Bone is the name of a **thing**.

A noun is the name of a person, animal or thing.

A   Make a list of the nouns shown in this picture.

B   Find the nouns in these sentences and write them down.

1   The car skidded on the ice and hit a tree.

2   Diamonds, rubies and emeralds are precious stones.

3   There are eleven players in a soccer team.

4   A dog is sometimes called "man's best friend".

5   The chief city of a country is called the capital.

6   The heart pumps blood to the body.

7   Rust is caused by oxygen in the air.

8   The referee ordered the offending player off the field.

C   Complete the nouns with missing letters.

1   A r e s _ _ _ _ _ _ _ _ is a place where you can buy and eat a meal.

2   A h _ _ _ _ _ _ _ _ _ is a kind of plane capable of rising straight up from the ground and hovering in the air.

3   An artist mixes colours on a p _ _ _ _ _ _ .

4   A tr _ _ _ _ _ _ has three sides and three angles.

5   A d _ _ _ _ _ is a banknote used in the United States of America.

Verbs

Jamal **washed** his face and **brushed** his hair.

The words **washed** and **brushed** are verbs.

A verb is a word which shows action.

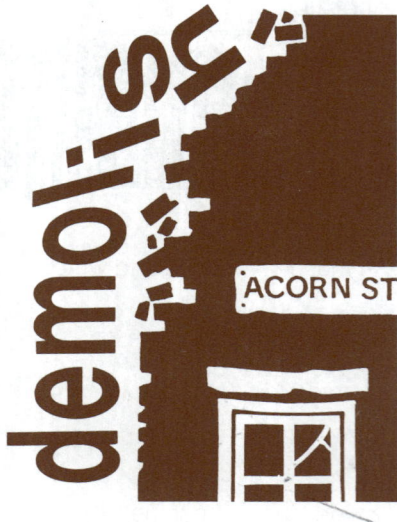

A Make a list of the verbs in these sentences.

1 Fish breathe through their gills.

2 Many animals hibernate during the winter.

3 Some of them wake and search for food on mild days.

4 After digging the garden, Dad raked it well.

5 Brazil produces and exports vast quantities of coffee.

6 The ship struck an iceberg and sank.

B Copy the verbs in the column on the left, then opposite each write the meaning from the list below which matches it. Use your dictionary to help.

apologize	1	to breathe in
bewilder	2	to eat like an animal
comprehend	3	to become less stiff or firm
confess	4	to tell as a secret
confide	5	to spend the winter asleep
demolish	6	to uncover; to lay open
devour	7	to express regret
discuss	8	to put out; to wipe out
expose	9	to work hard or try hard
extinguish	10	to understand
fortify	11	to make strong
glare	12	to pull or tear down
hibernate	13	to annoy; to irritate
inhale	14	to stare in anger
loathe	15	to confuse completely
meditate	16	to think quietly
pester	17	to own up to a sin
relax	18	to join together
strive	19	to talk over
unite	20	to regard with disgust

Adjectives

The captain had a **black bushy** beard.

The words **black** and **bushy** describe the captain's beard.

A word which describes a noun is called an adjective.

A Make a list of the adjectives in these sentences.

1 Rabbits become tame and affectionate when kept as pets.

2 Fruit for jam-making must be sound, ripe, dry and clean.

3 The Canadian prairies are vast plains where huge quantities of wheat are grown.

4 Tame mice are sociable but quarrelsome creatures.

5 The otter has short legs, webbed toes and thick fur.

6 To withstand rough winds, lighthouses are built of interlocking blocks of masonry.

B Copy the adjectives in the column on the left. Opposite each write the meaning from the list below which matches it. Use your dictionary to help.

arrogant	1	richly coloured; splendid
boisterous	2	giving a warm welcome
contemptuous	3	very scornful
distinguished	4	requiring much work
elaborate	5	boastfully proud
frantic	6	successful; thriving
gorgeous	7	well-known; famous
hospitable	8	heavy and clumsy
intelligent	9	bright; shining
laborious	10	quick at learning
memorable	11	self-important
obstinate	12	not moving
pompous	13	very noisy and disorderly
ponderous	14	worked out with great care
prosperous	15	not running or flowing
radiant	16	stubborn
repulsive	17	rough; violent
stagnant	18	causing strong dislike
stationary	19	not to be forgotten
tumultuous	20	wild with rage or pain

Adverbs

1 The troops fought **gallantly**.

   Gallantly tells **how** the troops fought. (*manner*)

2 We looked **everywhere** for the lost ball.

   Everywhere tells **where** we looked. (*place*)

3 We looked for the lost ball **yesterday**.

   Yesterday tells **when** we looked. (*time*)

A word which describes how, where or when an action is performed is called an adverb.

A   Make a list of the adverbs in these sentences. After each write **how**, **where** or **when** as required.

1 Nigel washed the dishes carefully.

2 Diana calls to see us frequently.

3 All the rabbits ran away.

4 The two boys wandered aimlessly round the town.

5 The train will be arriving shortly.

6 Dozens of rooks were cawing noisily.

B   Complete each sentence by using a suitable adverb from the column on the left. Use your dictionary to help.

awkwardly
bitterly
contentedly
courageously
frugally
gracefully
hungrily
intimately
merrily
mournfully
patiently
politely
soundly
uproariously
violently

1 The thief struggled ____ .
2 We waited ____ .
3 The robin chirped ____ .
4 The child wept ____ .
5 The old man fell ____ .
6 The champion fought ____ .
7 The miser lives ____ .
8 He ate his food ____ .
9 The cows grazed ____ .
10 He raised his hat ____ .
11 The wind howled ____ .
12 We all laughed ____ .
13 The girls danced ____ .
14 The baby slept ____ .
15 I know him ____ .

Nouns number

Singular	Plural
chief	chiefs
chimney	chimneys
deer	deer
diary	diaries
disco	discos
factory	factories
goose	geese
hero	heroes
man	men
mouse	mice
ox	oxen
photo	photos
piano	pianos
potato	potatoes
sheaf	sheaves
shelf	shelves
son-in-law	sons-in-law
thief	thieves
turkey	turkeys
wolf	wolves

A   Write the plurals of these words.

1	piano	6	diary	11	deer
2	sheaf	7	goose	12	disco
3	chimney	8	photo	13	factory
4	hero	9	thief	14	son-in-law
5	mouse	10	chief	15	man

B   Write the missing words.

1	factory	many ____
2	turkey	a flock of ____
3	chief	two ____
4	potato	a sack of ____
5	thief	a gang of ____
6	wolf	a pack of ____
7	piano	four ____
8	deer	a herd of ____
9	ox	a team of ____
10	mouse	three ____

C   Rewrite these sentences, changing the nouns in bold type to the plural number and making any other changes which may be necessary.

1   The **thief** removed the **turkey** from the **shelf**.

2   The **chief** put away his **knife**.

3   The **hero** had his **photo** taken.

4   The **child** looked at the little white **mouse**.

5   The **fox** looked longingly at the **goose**.

Attacked by a crow

The strange fragrance was stronger now, coming over the top of the rise in a wave of scent that struck him powerfully – as the scent of orange-blossom in the Mediterranean strikes a traveller who smells it for the first time. Fascinated, he ran to the crest. Nearby was another hedgerow and beyond, moving gently in the breeze, stood a field of broad beans in full flower.

Hazel squatted on his haunches and stared at the orderly forest of small, glaucous trees with their columns of black-and-white bloom. He had never seen anything like this. Wheat and barley he knew, and once he had been in a field of turnips. But this was entirely different from any of those and seemed, somehow, attractive, wholesome, propitious.

True, rabbits could not eat these plants: he could smell that. But they could lie safely among them for as long as they liked, and they could move through them easily and unseen. Hazel determined then and there to bring the rabbits up to the beanfield to shelter and rest until the evening. He ran back and found the others where he had left them. Bigwig and Silver were awake, but all the rest were still napping uneasily.

"Not asleep, Silver?" he said.

"It's too dangerous, Hazel," replied Silver. "I'd like to sleep as much as anyone, but if we all sleep and something comes, who's going to spot it?"

"I know. I've found a place where we can sleep safely for as long as we like."

"A burrow?"

"No, not a burrow. A great field of scented plants that will cover us, sight and smell, until we're rested. Come out here and smell it, if you like."

Both rabbits did so. "You say you've seen these plants?" said Bigwig, turning his ears to catch the distant rustling of the beans.

"Yes, they're only just over the top. Come on, let's get the others moving before a man comes with a *hrududu** or they'll scatter all over the place."

Silver roused the others and began to coax them into the field. They stumbled out drowsily, responding with reluctance to his repeated assurance that it was "only a little way".

They became widely separated as they struggled up the slope. Silver and Bigwig led the way, with Hazel and Buckthorn a short distance behind. The rest idled along, hopping a few yards and then pausing to nibble or to pass droppings on the warm, sunny grass.

Silver was almost at the crest when suddenly, from half-way up, there came a high screaming – the sound a rabbit makes, not to call for help or frighten an enemy, but simply out of terror. Fiver and Pipkin, limping behind the others, and conspicuously undersized and

*Tractor – or any motor.

tired, were being attacked by the crow. It had flown low along the ground. Then, pouncing, it had aimed a blow of its great bill at Fiver, who just managed to dodge in time. Now it was leaping and hopping among the grass tussocks, striking at the two rabbits with terrible darts of its head. Crows aim at the eyes and Pipkin, sensing this, had buried his head in a clump of rank grass and was trying to burrow farther in. It was he who was screaming.

Hazel covered the distance down the slope in a few seconds. He had no idea what he was going to do and if the crow had ignored him he would probably have been at a loss. But by dashing up he distracted its attention and it turned on him. He swerved past it, stopped and, looking back, saw Bigwig come racing in from the opposite side. The crow turned again, struck at Bigwig and missed. Hazel heard its beak hit a pebble in the grass with a sound like a snail-shell when a thrush beats it on a stone. As Silver followed Bigwig, it recovered itself and faced him squarely. Silver stopped short in fear and the crow seemed to dance before him, its great, black wings flapping in a horrible commotion. It was just about to stab when Bigwig ran straight into it from behind and knocked it sideways …

Watership Down   Richard Adams

1   In what way was the scent of the beanfield like the scent of orange-blossom in the Mediterranean?
2   What colour are the broad bean flowers?
3   Give two reasons why it would be safe for the rabbits to sleep in the beanfield.
4   Which two rabbits had been keeping watch while the younger rabbits tried to sleep?
5   Which rabbit was the closest to the beanfield when the crow attacked Pipkin and Fiver?
6   Why had the crow chosen Pipkin and Fiver for attack?
7   With what did the crow aim at Fiver?
8   How did Pipkin attempt to escape the crow's attack?
9   Who ran to Pipkin's aid?
0   In what way did this action assist Pipkin?
1   To what does the writer compare the sound made by the crow's beak on the pebble?
2   Which two creatures stood face to face in this fight?
3   What stopped the crow from stabbing at Silver?

Verbs past tense and past participles

Remember
The **past tense** of a verb does **not** need a helping word (an auxiliary verb).

Example
All the ponds **froze** last night.

The **past participle** always requires an auxiliary verb.

Example
All the ponds **are frozen** this morning.

Auxiliary verbs
is
are
was
were
has
have
having
had
be
been
being
am

Present tense	Past tense	Past participle
bear	bore	borne
beat	beat	beaten
begin	began	begun
blow	blew	blown
break	broke	broken
burst	burst	burst
choose	chose	chosen
deal	dealt	dealt
drive	drove	driven
drown	drowned	drowned
fight	fought	fought
flee	fled	fled
freeze	froze	frozen
go	went	gone
hang *(thing)*	hung	hung
hang *(person)*	hanged	hanged
hurt	hurt	hurt
lay	laid	laid
lie	lay	lain
mistake	mistook	mistaken
show	showed	shown
slay	slew	slain
think	thought	thought
weave	wove	woven
wring	wrung	wrung

A   In each sentence below insert the **past tense** of the verb in bold type.

1   Tom and John ____ a gruelling fight.   **fight**

2   The defeated army ____ before their pursuers.   **flee**

3   The gladiator ____ his opponent with his sword.   **slay**

4   On reaching home Veronica ____ the table for tea.   **lay**

5   Dad ____ his hand with an electric drill.   **hurt**

6   The spider ____ a web in a very short time.   **weave**

7   His teacher ____ him for his twin
brother.   **mistake**

8   Vast floods ____ hundreds of sheep
yesterday.   **drown**

B   Copy each sentence and complete by inserting
the **past participle** of the verb in bold type.

1   We rested after our visitors had ____ .   **go**

2   He had ____ of a good answer to the
question.   **think**

3   Several passengers were ____ in the
collision.   **hurt**

4   David was ____ to captain the school
team.   **choose**

5   This lovely scarf was ____ by hand.   **weave**

6   The condemned man was ____ at eight o'clock in
the morning.   **hang**

7   Margaret did the sum after her teacher had ____ her
the right method.   **show**

8   The ground was ____ so the match was
postponed.   **freeze**

C   Insert in each space either the **past tense** or
the **past participle** of the verb in bold type, as
required.

1   The patient ____ the pain without flinching.   **bear**

2   The old ship is to be ____ up next month.   **break**

3   Many trees were ____ down during the
gale.   **blow**

4   Work was ____ on the new school
yesterday.   **begin**

5   The winner ____ the racing car skilfully.   **drive**

6   Our team will probably be ____ in the final.   **beat**

7   After lunch Grandma ____ down to rest.   **lie**

8   Barbara washed the towel and ____ it out.   **wring**

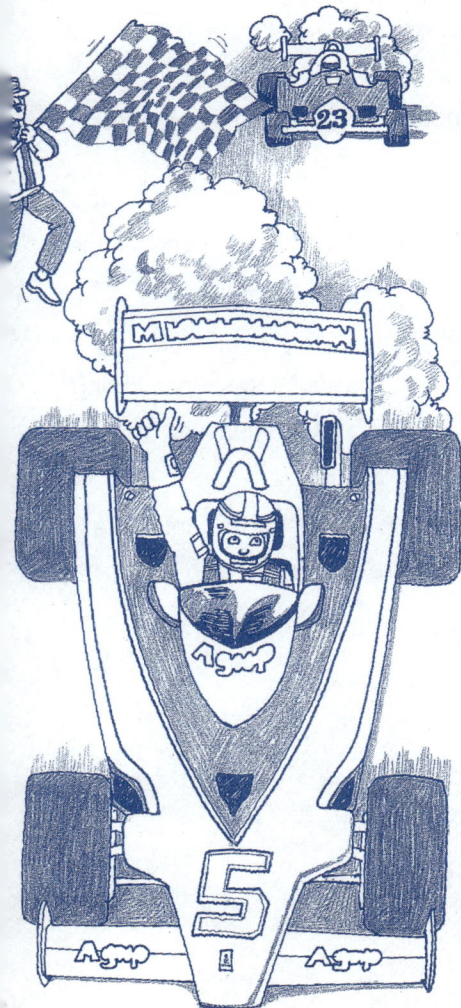

Sentences, clauses and phrases

Look at this group of words.
Mr. Dobbin bought a new sports car yesterday.

Does it make complete sense?
Yes.
Does it contain a verb? Yes

Then it is a **sentence**.

A sentence is a group of words which make complete sense. Every sentence contains a verb.

Look at this group of words.
Which had new tyres

Does it make complete sense?
No.
Does it contain a verb? Yes.

Then it is a **clause**.

Look at this group of words.
Without even a glance at his book

Does it make complete sense?
No.
Does it contain a verb? No.

Then it is a **phrase**.

A Say whether each group of words is a sentence, a clause or a phrase.

1 Most trees shed their leaves every autumn.

2 Early in the autumn of every year

3 Whenever they can

4 Most people work.

5 The farmer chased the boys.

6 Who were very frightened

7 Dogs with long hair and broad feet

8 Dogs bark.

B Form a sentence from each clause and phrase below.

1 . . . . at the bus stop.

2 . . . . because she is very fond of chocolates.

3 With one shot . . . .

4 Although he was very ill . . . .

5 . . . . on our doorstep every morning.

6 . . . . whenever she can.

7 With great pride . . . .

8 . . . . who has climbed Mount Everest.

9 . . . . who are bullies . . . .

10 Thinking quickly . . . .

Nouns gender

Masculine	Feminine
boar	sow
brother	sister
buck	doe
bull	cow
colt	filly
drake	duck
emperor	empress
heir	heiress
host	hostess
husband	wife
lord	lady
marquis	marchioness
mayor	mayoress
nephew	niece
peacock	peahen
ram	ewe
sir	madam
stag	hind
stallion	mare
widower	widow
wizard	witch

A   Write the **feminine** gender of:

1	sir	6	emperor
2	stallion	7	marquis
3	lord	8	bull
4	mayor	9	nephew
5	peacock	10	heir

B   Write the **masculine** gender of:

1	duck	6	filly
2	sow	7	niece
3	widow	8	ewe
4	witch	9	doe
5	hind	10	empress

C   In each sentence change the **masculine** noun to the **feminine** gender. You may need to change other words too.

1   The Emperor had twenty sons.

2   A beautiful peacock strutted about the lawn.

3   The driver of the bus was a young man.

4   The rich uncle sent a handsome present to his nephew.

5   The marquis is cruising in the Mediterranean.

6   The letter began, "Dear Sir".

D   Complete each sentence by using a noun of the opposite gender to that in bold type.

1   Farmer Bond keeps two **bulls** and eight _____ .

2   The **drake** swam on the pond while the _____ waddled round the farmyard with her little ones.

3   A record price was paid for the _____ and the **cow**.

4   **Lord** and _____ Bryce were at the garden party.

5   The wool on the **ram** was thicker than that on the _____ .

6   The red deer **stag** had antlers; the _____ had none.

Toad and company

When they were quite ready the now triumphant Toad led his companions to the paddock and set them to capture the old grey horse, who, without having been consulted, and to his own extreme annoyance, had been told off by Toad for the dustiest job in this dusty expedition. He frankly preferred the paddock, and took a great deal of catching. Meantime Toad packed the lockers still tighter with necessaries, and hung nose-bags, nets of onions, bundles of hay, and baskets from the bottom of the cart. At last the horse was caught and harnessed, and they set off, all talking at once, each animal either trudging by the side of the cart or sitting on the shaft, as the humour took him. It was a golden afternoon. The smell of the dust they kicked up was rich and satisfying; out of thick orchards on either side of the road birds called and whistled to them cheerily; good-natured passers-by gave them "Good day," or stopped to say nice things about their beautiful cart; and rabbits, sitting at their front doors in the hedgerows, held up their fore-paws and said, "O my! O my! O my!"

Late in the evening, tired and happy and miles from home, they drew up on a remote common far from habitations, turned the horse loose to graze, and ate their simple supper sitting on the grass by the side of the cart. Toad talked big about all he was going to do in the days to come, while stars grew fuller and larger all around them, and a yellow moon, appearing suddenly and silently from nowhere in particular, came to keep them company and listen to their talk. At last they turned into their little bunks in the cart; and Toad, kicking out his legs, sleepily said, "Well, good night, you fellows! This is the real life for a gentleman! Talk about your old river!"

"I *don't* talk about my river," replied the patient Rat. "You *know* I don't, Toad. But I *think* about it," he added pathetically, in a lower tone: "I *think* about it – all the time!"

The Mole reached out from under his blanket, felt for the Rat's paw in the darkness, and gave it a squeeze. "I'll do whatever you like, Ratty," he whispered. "Shall we run away tomorrow morning, quite early – *very* early – and go back to our dear old hole on the river?"

"No, no, we'll see it out," whispered back the Rat. "Thanks awfully, but I ought to stick by Toad till this trip is ended. It wouldn't be safe for him to be left to himself. It won't take very long. His fads never do. Good night!"

The end was indeed nearer than even the Rat suspected.

After so much open air and excitement the Toad slept very soundly, and no amount of shaking could rouse him out of bed next morning. So the Mole and Rat turned to, quietly and manfully, and while the Rat saw to the horse, and lit a fire, and cleaned last night's cups and platters, and got things ready for breakfast, the Mole trudged off to the nearest village, a long way off, for milk and eggs and various necessaries the Toad had, of course, forgotten to provide. The hard work had all been done, and the two animals were resting, thoroughly exhausted, by the time Toad appeared on the scene, fresh and gay, remarking what a pleasant easy life it was they were all leading now, after the cares and worries and fatigues of housekeeping at home.

The Wind in the Willows   Kenneth Grahame

1   What job did Toad give Rat and Mole to do while he packed the lockers?
2   What made Rat and Mole's job difficult to do?
3   What did Toad hang from the bottom of the cart?
4   What were the animals doing when they were not trudging by the side of the cart?
5   Where did Toad and his friends stop for the night?
6   What did they do with the horse?
7   Where did they eat their supper?
8   Write down one word that means the same as **talked big** in the second paragraph.
9   How do we know that Rat is feeling a little homesick?
10   Why doesn't he leave Toad and go straight home?
11   Who sets off to buy what they need for breakfast?
12   Do you think Rat and Mole would agree with Toad when he comments on the "pleasant easy life" they are leading?
13   Write down five adjectives that would describe Toad accurately on the evidence of this extract from *The Wind in the Willows*.

Adjectives formation

Some adjectives are formed simply by adding the letter **y** to a noun.

Examples cloud   cloudy
mould   mouldy
marsh   marshy

When the noun ends with **e**, this letter is dropped before the **y** is added.

Examples shade   shady
smoke   smoky
juice   juicy

When **y** is added to some nouns the last letter is doubled.

Examples sun   sunny
mud   muddy
star   starry

A Use the adjective formed from the noun in bold type to fill each space. Copy the phrases in your book.

1 A material covered with **fluff**   a _____ material
2 A voice with a **squeak**   a _____ voice
3 Foods containing much **starch**   _____ foods
4 A man of great **wealth**   a _____ man
5 A morning with much **frost**   a _____ morning

B Insert in each space the adjective formed from the noun in bold type. Remember to drop the final **e**.

1 A path with many **stones**   a _____ path
2 Hair in which there is a **wave**   _____ hair
3 Dishes covered with **grease**   _____ dishes
4 A day when a **breeze** is blowing   a _____ day
5 A dinner with a nice **taste**   a _____ dinner
6 A beach covered with **pebbles**   a _____ beach

C Form the adjective from the noun in bold type to fill each space. Remember to double the final letter.

1 An animal covered with **fur**   a _____ animal
2 A sound like that of **tin**   a _____ sound
3 Wood full of **knots**   _____ wood
4 Land which is largely **bog**   _____ land
5 A speech containing much **wit**   a _____ speech
6 A hand which is more **skin** than flesh   a _____ hand

D Form the adjective from the noun in bold type. You need to remember all the rules for forming adjectives for this exercise.

1 roads covered in **ice**   _____ roads
2 hair like **wire**   _____ hair
3 a complexion with **spots**   a _____ complexion
4 sunshine through **haze**   _____ sunshine
5 a beach of **sand**   a _____ beach
6 a morning of **fog**   a _____ morning

Nouns formation

Verb	Noun
abolish	abolition
accuse	accusation
advise	advice
astonish	astonishment
choose	choice
complain	complaint
complete	completion
deceive	deceit
decide	decision
destroy	destruction
explain	explanation
explode	explosion
favour	favouritism
imagine	imagination
improve	improvement
inquire	inquiry
pronounce	pronunciation
pursue	pursuit
satisfy	satisfaction

The nouns here are all **abstract nouns**. They are the names of ideas and feelings.

A Copy these phrases, inserting in the spaces the nouns formed from the verbs in bold type.

1 a lively ____ **imagine**
2 sound ____ **advise**
3 a violent ____ **explode**
4 widespread ____ **destroy**
5 blatant ____ **favour**
6 complete ____ **astonish**
7 a sensible ____ **decide**
8 correct ____ **pronounce**
9 a false ____ **accuse**
10 a serious ____ **complain**

B Complete each sentence by inserting the noun formed from the verb in bold type.

1 Purchasers have a ____ of several colours. **choose**

2 In 1833 an Act was passed for the ____ of slavery in the British Empire. **abolish**

3 Any ____ to increase pensions will be welcomed. **decide**

4 He listened patiently to his teacher's ____ . **explain**

5 The work was done to the customer's ____ . **satisfy**

6 Several hunters went in ____ of the lion. **pursue**

7 An ____ is a search for truth, knowledge or information. **inquire**

8 The work on the new road is nearing ____ . **complete**

9 ____ means making a person believe to be true something which is false. **deceive**

10 The ____ in Jake's written work was amazing. **improve**

Other words for said and asked

Using **said** or **asked** too often makes your writing monotonous.

Choose the most suitable word from the list on the left to complete each sentence.

A

admitted
announced
boasted
remarked
shouted
stammered
urged
whispered

1 "It is much colder today than it was yesterday," ____ the old boatman.

2 "Hush, Becky," ____ her mother, "or you will wake the baby."

3 "Go on, Samran," ____ his teacher, "try to beat David's jump."

4 "All hands on deck," ____ the skipper of the trawler.

5 "I b-b-beg your pardon," ____ the frightened boy.

6 "Yes, it was I who broke the basin," ____ Kai Man.

7 "I am easily the best reader in the class," ____ Alan.

8 "The school will be closed all next week," ____ the headmaster.

B

complained
grumbled
inquired
ordered
pleaded
prophesied
protested
replied

1 "Prepare the theatre for an emergency operation at once," ____ the surgeon.

2 "Is this the way to the Post Office, please?" ____ the stranger.

3 "Yes," ____ the policeman, "keep straight on for about fifty metres and you will see it on your left."

4 "Please, Mum, may I have just one more chocolate?" ____ Elizabeth.

5 "Your prices are far too high," ____ the customer to the grocer.

6 "I think we are going to have a very warm summer this year," ____ Aunt Jane.

7 "Your dog has been worrying my sheep, Mr. Bath," ____ the farmer.

8 "I get all the tedious jobs," ____ the shop assistant.

Collective nouns

actors	company
angels	host
arrows	sheaf; quiver
bells	peal
chicks	brood
directors	board
eggs	clutch
golf-clubs	set
lions	pride
locusts	plague; swarm
magistrates	bench
minstrels	troupe
pilgrims	band
thieves	gang
singers	choir
spectators	crowd
stars	cluster; galaxy
swallows	flight
teachers	staff
trees	clump
worshippers	congregation

Write the missing words.

A

1 a _____ of singers
2 a _____ of teachers
3 a _____ of chicks
4 a _____ of bells
5 a _____ of actors
6 a _____ of locusts
7 a _____ of spectators
8 a _____ of thieves
9 a _____ of lions
10 a _____ of swallows

B

1 a host of _____
2 a clump of _____
3 a cluster of _____
4 a band of _____
5 a board of _____
6 a troupe of _____
7 a quiver of _____
8 a bench of_____
9 a congregation of _____
10 a clutch of _____

C   Write the collective nouns needed to complete these sentences.

1 The _____ of pilgrims halted before the mosque.

2 A _____ of locusts devoured every growing plant.

3 The mother hen was accompanied by her _____ of chicks.

4 Under a small _____ of trees a tent had been pitched.

5 Several plays have been performed by this brilliant _____ of actors.

6 The police are searching for a _____ of car thieves.

7 The _____ of directors met to consider their company's losses.

8 The match was watched by a huge _____ of spectators.

9 In his dream Jacob saw a _____ of angels.

10 The children saw a _____ of swallows making for the sea.

11 The _____ in the tiny chapel prayed silently.

12 My grandfather was given a _____ of golf-clubs when he retired.

Wildlife in danger

It is a disturbing fact that today many different kinds of wild animal throughout the world are in danger of extinction. The reasons for this are many and varied, but we must largely blame pollution, pesticides, the disturbance of the animals' natural environment and man's greed and thoughtlessness.

Industry has grown enormously, and it has become common practice for factories to dispose of waste matter in streams and rivers, causing great loss of river life. Modern agricultural methods include the use of pesticides which effectively control insects classified as pests, but which also destroy many that are not. An increase in population has meant more building – and with it the destruction of much of the countryside that provides habitat for wild animals. To satisfy man's selfish desires the polar bear in North America is under threat, hunted by sportsmen; in Borneo and Sumatra the orang-utan has become part of a smuggling racket; in South America the chinchilla is almost extinct because its fur is in demand; whales are massacred world-wide for the oil and food they yield. These are only a few of the species under threat.

But the problem is receiving world-wide recognition, and some action is being taken. To name a few examples – sewage pollution in the River Thames has been greatly reduced; a ban on trading in some furs has been agreed; and organisations like Friends of the Earth do valuable work in this deserving cause.

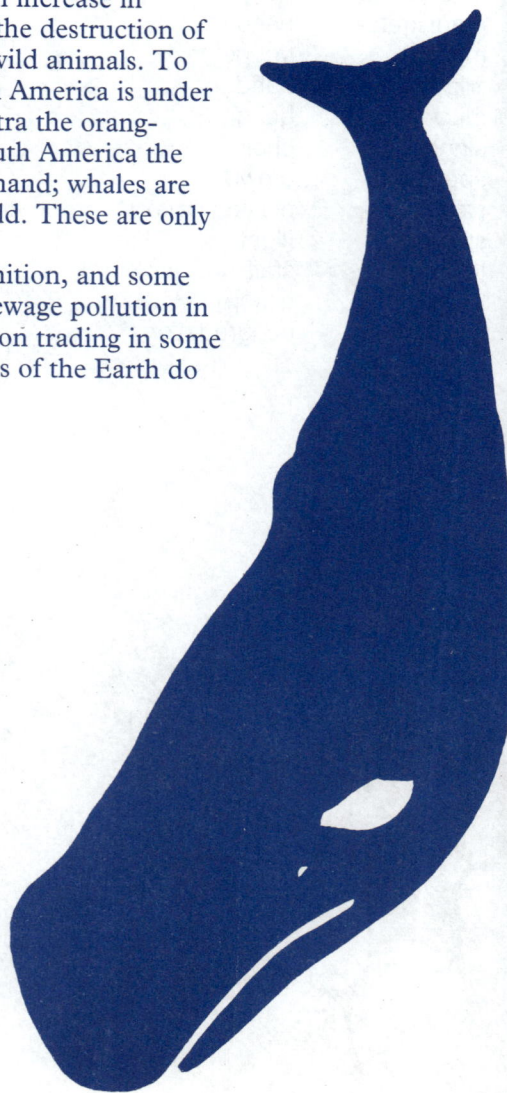

1   Give in your own words two reasons why some species of wild animal may become extinct.
2   How do factories contribute to the problem?
3   What is the meaning of **pesticide**?
4   What effect has the increase in the human population had upon wildlife?
5   Why is the polar bear in North America under threat?
6   Which countries have problems with smuggling?
7   Which animal is hunted for its fur?
8   Why are whales hunted in such large numbers?
9   What is being done to help preserve our river life?
10 Name one other way in which wildlife is currently helped.
11 Provide a subtitle for each paragraph that will sum up what each is about.

Fun with words

a _ _ _ _   a male farm animal

b _ _ _ _ _ _   a missile fired from
               a rifle

Word (**a**) is bull

Word (**b**) is bullet

Now try the exercise below. Remember that each dash stands for a letter, and that the second word of each pair is formed by adding letters to the first word.

A

1. **a** _ _ _ _   a large stringed instrument
   b _ _ _ _ _ _ _   a spear used in hunting whales

2. **a** _ _ _ _   a man who lives in a monastery
   b _ _ _ _ _ _   an agile and mischievous animal

3. **a** _ _ _   a young goat
   b _ _ _ _ _ _   to steal a person by force

4. **a** _ _ _   an article of headgear
   b _ _ _ _ _ _ _   a small axe

5. **a** _ _ _ _   an American coin of small value
   b _ _ _ _ _ _   the middle

6. **a** _ _ _ _   a place where ships can shelter
   b _ _ _ _ _ _ _   a part or a share

7. **a** _ _ _ _   stop
   b _ _ _ _ _ _   a rope or strap for leading an animal

8. **a** _ _ _ _   a man who entertains guests
   b _ _ _ _ _ _ _   of an enemy; unfriendly

9. **a** _ _ _   a male child
   b _ _ _ _ _ _ _   to refuse to have anything to do with

10. **a** _ _ _ _   a lump; a large quantity together
    b _ _ _ _ _ _ _ _   wholesale pitiless slaughter

B

In a certain code
the figures   **5 2 9 7 4 6 3 1 8**
stand for the word   C O M P A N I E S

Write the words for: Write the figures for:

1	**8**	**5**	**4**	**9**	**7**		6	C	A	P	E	S
2	**5**	**2**	**9**	**1**	**8**		7	O	P	E	N	S
3	**7**	**4**	**6**	**3**	**5**		8	S	P	I	C	E
4	**8**	**6**	**3**	**7**	**1**		9	P	I	A	N	O
5	**8**	**7**	**4**	**5**	**1**		10	S	C	O	N	E

19

Using the right adjective

A Copy the adjectives in column **a** in your exercise book in the order given. Opposite each write the noun in column **b** which matches it.

a	b
frantic	slope
antique	allowance
affectionate	drugs
formidable	grip
palatable	clothes
injurious	daughter
threadbare	struggles
meagre	task
precipitous	furniture
relentless	meal

B Choose the word from the list on the left which will complete each sentence correctly.

shrewd
vivid
candid
riotous
abundant
luscious
secluded
righteous
sumptuous
prosperous

1   The traveller had many ___ memories of his jungle adventures.

2   The peach is a ___ fruit.

3   Sir Walter is the managing director of a ___ business.

4   The ___ businessman made a profit.

5   A ___ feast was held in the emperor's honour.

6   The boys were rocking with ___ laughter.

7   The town is proud of its ___ supply of water.

8   He gave them his ___ opinion of their actions.

9   At the bottom of the garden was a ___ nook with an oak seat beneath a shady tree.

10   The insult filled the woman with ___ indignation.

Pronouns

a John told Susan that John would lend Susan a book.

b John told Susan that **he** would lend **her** a book.

Instead of repeating the word John, the word **he** is used in (**b**).

Instead of repeating the word **Susan**, the word **her** is used.

A word which is used instead of a noun is called a pronoun.

herself

her   itself

it

he
it
we
us
she
her
his
him
them
they

A   Rewrite these sentences, using pronouns from the list on the left in place of the words in bold type.

1 Anne told Justine that **Anne** would knit a cardigan for **Justine**.

2 When Colin was given a dog **Colin** trained **the dog** to walk to heel.

3 Ramu and I are good friends. **Ramu and I** go everywhere together.

4 As Roger and I approached the farmyard gate a big dog barked at **Roger and me**.

5 The teacher sent for Robin and Alan. **The teacher** told **Robin and Alan** to stay in after school.

6 The two girls knew that **the two girls** would be late.

7 Andrew was sad because the stolen bicycle was **Andrew's**.

B   Insert one of the pronouns in the list on the left in each sentence.

myself
itself
yourself
ourselves
yourselves
herself

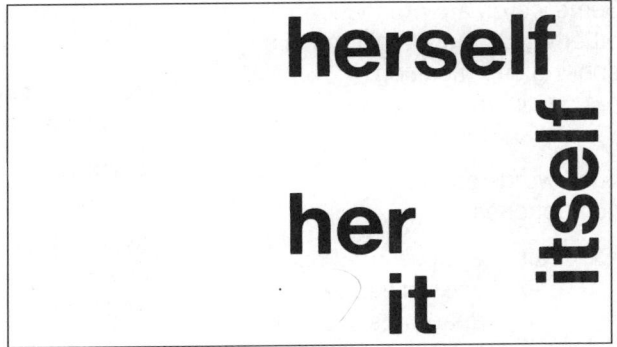

1 You boys must make _____ useful in the garden.

2 Did you make this table_____ , Spencer?

3 The hedgehog can roll _____ into a prickly ball.

4 I can work the sum by _____ , thank you.

5 Leela certainly thinks _____ somebody of importance.

6 We built the house _____ .

Homophones

Some words are pronounced like other words but are different in spelling and meaning,
e.g. main, mane
bear, bare.

Such words are called homophones.

air	what we breathe
heir	one entitled to a dead person's property
allowed	permitted
aloud	loud enough to be heard
beach	the sea-shore
beech	a tree
boy	a male child
buoy	a floating marker for ships
brake	a device to check speed
break	to cause something to come into pieces
cereal	wheat, barley and oats are all cereals
serial	a story or film appearing in parts
check	to stop; a squared pattern
cheque	an order to a bank to pay money
coarse	rough
course	a track; an onward movement
currant	a dried grape
current	a flow of water, air, etc.
foul	filthy; wicked; vile
fowl	a bird

A Choose the correct word from the pair above to complete each sentence.

1 **cereal   serial**
Cornflakes are his favourite ____ .

2 **currant   current**
These ____ buns are delicious.

3 **foul   fowl**
Fulham were awarded a free-kick for a ____ on their goalkeeper.

4 **air   heir**
Prince Charles is ____ to the throne.

5 **break   brake**
New blocks had to be fitted to the front ____ of the bicycle.

B Write five pairs of words to complete these sentences.

1 Dad paid by ____ for his new ____ suit.

2 The ____ who fell overboard swam to a nearby ____ .

3 Talking ____ is not ____ in the reading room of the library.

4 Racing was difficult because the grass on the ____ was long and ____ .

5 Not far from the sandy ____ grew a clump of ____ trees.

Abbreviations

Abbreviations are shortened forms of words or phrases.

Learn this list, then do the exercises.

A.A.	Automobile Association
a.s.a.p.	as soon as possible
c/o	care of
Dept.	Department
H.R.H.	His (Her) Royal Highness
J.P.	Justice of the Peace
Ltd.	Limited
M.D.	Managing Director
M.P.	Member of Parliament
n/a	not applicable; not available
N.S.P.C.C.	National Society for the Prevention of Cruelty to Children
O.H.M.S.	On Her Majesty's Service
R.N.	Royal Navy
R.S.P.C.A.	Royal Society for the Prevention of Cruelty to Animals
U.N.	United Nations
Tel.	Telephone

A Write the meanings of the abbreviations in bold type.

1 The widow wrote to her **M.P.** about her compensation.

2 The letter was addressed to the Sales **Dept.**

3 An inspector of the **N.S.P.C.C.** called to inspect the house.

4 Tim's holiday address is **c/o** Mrs. Baines, 15 High St., Burland.

5 A large crowd gathered to greet **H.R.H.** Princess Margaret.

6 The matter has been reported to the **R.S.P.C.A.**

7 Please reply **a.s.a.p.**

8 The warrant for the arrest of the culprit was signed by a **J.P.**

B Give the meaning of each abbreviation in bold type.

1 On the notepaper was printed: **Tel.** Bury 2385.

2 No postage is payable on letters and parcels sent **O.H.M.S.**

3 The building of the **R.N.** Barracks at Devonport was begun in 1879.

4 The **A.A.** was founded in London in 1905.

5 Both Britain and America are members of the **U.N.**

6 Mum's company has a new **M.D.**

C Use your dictionary to find out what these abbreviations stand for.

1 fax
2 G.P.
3 R.I.P
4 anon.
5 H.Q.

Rikki-tikki and Darzee

Then Rikki-tikki went out into the garden to see what was to be seen. It was a large garden, only half-cultivated, with bushes as big as summer-houses of Marshal Niel roses, lime and orange trees, clumps of bamboo, and thickets of high grass. Rikki-tikki licked his lips. "This is a splendid hunting-ground," he said, and his tail grew bottle-brushy at the thought of it, and he scuttled up and down the garden, snuffing here and there till he heard very sorrowful voices in a thornbush.

It was Darzee, the tailor-bird, and his wife. They had made a beautiful nest by pulling two big leaves together and stitching them up the edges with fibres, and had filled the hollow with cotton and downy fluff. The nest swayed to and fro, as they sat on the rim and cried.

"What is the matter?" asked Rikki-tikki.

"We are very miserable," said Darzee. "One of our babies fell out of the nest yesterday, and Nag ate him."

"H'm!" said Rikki-tikki. "That is very sad – but I am a stranger here. Who is Nag?"

Darzee and his wife only cowered down in the nest without answering, for from the thick grass at the foot of the bush there came a low hiss – a horrid cold sound that made Rikki-tikki jump back two clear feet. Then inch by inch out of the grass rose up the head and spread hood of Nag, the big black cobra, and he was five feet long from tongue to tail.

The Jungle Book   Rudyard Kipling

1 Why did Rikki-tikki lick his lips?
2 What change came over Rikki-tikki's tail as he thought about this?
3 What did Rikki-tikki hear as he scuttled up and down the garden?
4 Explain why **tailor-bird** is an appropriate name for these birds.
5 Why were Darzee and his wife crying?
6 Where did the low hiss come from?
7 What did Darzee and his wife do when they heard this noise?
8 What effect did this sound have on Rikki-tikki?
9 How long was Nag from tongue to tail?
10 Write a list of all the facts about the cobra in this passage.

Letter writing

Alastair Brooks saw this advertisement in a magazine.

FREE

The REX packet of 100 foreign stamps to applicants for our approval sheets and illustrated catalogue.

Enclose stamp for postage.
Rex Stamp Co. Ltd., 146 Forsyth Rd., London NW5 2BQ

Rex Stamp Co. Ltd.,
146 Forsyth Road,
London
NW5 2BQ

Rex Stamp Co. Ltd.,
146 Forsyth Road,
London
NW5 2BQ

19 Jubilee Road,
Granton,
Kent
GN7 4CP

Dear Sirs,

Please send me the Rex free packet of foreign stamps, also a selection of approval sheets and a copy of your illustrated catalogue.

I enclose stamps for postage.

Yours faithfully,

Alastair Brooks.

This is how he addressed the envelope.

This is the letter he wrote.

Points to remember:

a Keep to the form of letter shown, giving your full address.

b State exactly what you require, making your letter as brief as possible.

c If requested to enclose stamps or a postal order, make sure you do so.

d Address the envelope plainly and fully, and see that it bears a stamp for the correct postage.

1 Write a letter to the Planet Novelty Co. Ltd, 49 Greenham Avenue, London E12 SA16 for a copy of their price-list of conjuring tricks, enclosing stamps for postage.

2 The Medico Co. Ltd., Grove Buildings, Anson Street, Birmingham B12 4EH, offer a free sample tube of Atlas toothpaste to all applicants enclosing stamps for postage. Send for a sample.

3 Write to the Mekko Model Co. Ltd., 37 Bilton Road, London SE16 8RL for a copy of their illustrated catalogue of model railways, aircraft, racing cars and boats, which will be sent post free.

Occupations

A   Write the names of these occupations.

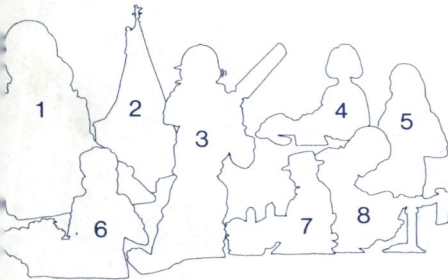

announcer   plumber
chef   butcher
florist   chemist
nurse   waitress
jeweller   steeplejack
librarian   tobacconist
cricketer   undertaker
coastguard   upholsterer
glazier   tailor

B   Select the word from the list on the left which will complete each sentence.

1   The ____ at the public library has three excellent assistants.

2   The ____ at the corner sells lots of different sweets and chocolates.

3   The ____ at the beach café served us with tea very quickly.

4   The ____ had a large selection of medicines and pills.

5   The ____ offered Maya a gold watch at a reduced price.

6   The twins went to the ____ to buy their mother a bouquet of flowers.

7   The ____ displays all the meat on trays in the shop window.

8   The ____ climbed to the top of the church steeple to inspect the damage done by the gale.

9   The ____ alerted the lifeboat crew.

10   The ____ took Tom's temperature and pulse every four hours.

Group names

A   Give the name of the group to which these objects belong.

B   Choose the word in the column on the left which belongs to each of the groups below. Give the name of each group.

Example   1   **venison**   names of meats

baker
silver
alligator
synagogue
villa
venison

1	beef	2	cathedral	3	cobra
	chicken		temple		crocodile
	lamb		church		adder
	mutton		chapel		lizard
4	house	5	copper	6	grocer
	bungalow		gold		butcher
	mansion		iron		fruiterer
	cottage		lead		fishmonger

C   Draw four columns and write the headings:

Clothes   Vessels   Furniture   Footwear

Then place the words below in their correct groups. There will be six words in each group.

liner	sandals	tights	wardrobe
clogs	submarine	boots	trousers
cupboard	scarf	sideboard	cruiser
shirt	armchair	yacht	cabinet
trawler	shoes	vest	wellingtons
table	schooner	slippers	jeans

Comparing adjectives

There are **three** degrees of adjectives.

1 The **positive degree**.
Used for one person or thing e.g. tall

2 The **comparative degree**.
Used in comparing two persons or things e.g. taller

3 The **superlative degree**.
Used in comparing more than two persons or things e.g. tallest

We can add **-er** and **-est** to many adjectives without any change in spelling, e.g. strong, stronger, strongest.

But look out for these spelling changes.

a Dropping final **e**.
e.g. wide, wider, widest

b Changing **y** to **i**.
e.g. happy, happier, happiest

c Doubling the last letter.
e.g. hot, hotter, hottest.

When comparing longer adjectives the words **more** and **most**, or **less** and **least** are placed before them.

Example
Jill is the **most reliable** person for the job.

Clare is **fast**.   Kelly is **faster**.

A Copy and complete this table.

Positive degree	Comparative degree	Superlative degree
1 lovely	____	____
2 large	____	____
3 hot	____	____
4 noisy	____	____
5 slim	____	____
6 wise	____	____
7 wet	____	____
8 wealthy	____	____
9 fine	____	____
10 greedy	____	____

B Complete each sentence, using the **comparative degree** or the **superlative degree** of the adjective in bold type.

1 Sanjay is the ____ pupil of the two.   **capable**

2 She is easily the ____ girl in the whole school.   **intelligent**

3 Julian is the ____ of the two brothers.   **generous**

4 Janna chose the ___ dress in the shop. **expensive**

5 A miner's work is ___ than a farmer's. **dangerous**

6 Many people consider the Taj Mahal to be the ___ building in the world. **wonderful**

7 The manager has the ___ job in the works. **important**

8 This is the ___ book of the two. **interesting**

Neelam is the **fastest**.

Some adjectives cannot be compared in the ways shown; they are irregular.

Positive degree	Comparative degree	Superlative degree
good	better	best
bad	worse	worst
ill	worse	worst
many	more	most
much	more	most
little	less	least

C Write the correct degree of the adjective which will complete each sentence.

1 This is the ___ blizzard I have ever seen. **bad**

2 The patient was very ill yesterday but he is even ___ today. **ill**

3 Both boys read well, but David is the ___ reader. **good**

4 Your cold is ___ than mine. **bad**

5 Kate is the ___ singer in the school choir. **good**

6 August is the month when guest-houses have the ___ bookings. **many**

7 £1 is the ___ amount that can be invested. **small**

8 Ahmed has little money; Paul has even ___ . **little**

William's workshop

SCENE 1   **On the way home from school**

Characters: LAURA, DANNY, WILLIAM

(William enters, looking fearfully behind him. He has a school bag on his back. He is followed by Danny and Laura.)

LAURA: Wimpy William! Wimpy William!

DANNY: He'll run away in a minute. Just watch him. Why don't you run away, wimp?

WILLIAM: I won't run away.

LAURA: Oh! He's being brave today. Go on, tell us about your workshop again, William. Tell us what you make in there.

DANNY: *(Sarcastically)* Didn't you know? William makes incredible things in there. He makes computers that talk to you and do your homework. And robot dogs that bark and fetch your slippers. He makes all sorts of wonderful stuff in there. He's a brilliant genius, an inventor. At least, that's what he's always telling us.

LAURA: *(Sarcastically)* Oh, I didn't know that. I didn't know he was a genius. I thought he was a little wimpy baby who can't fight, who runs away. I thought he was a daydreamer, like teacher says.

DANNY: And I thought he was a great big liar – who says he's inventing things in his workshop when he isn't.

WILLIAM: It's true, it's true. I do invent things. But they don't always work. I mean, I never said they worked, did I?

LAURA: He's making excuses now!

WILLIAM: I'm not, I'm just…

DANNY: *(Interrupting)* Well, I think it's about time we saw one of these wonderful inventions. Go on, William, bring in your latest invention. Bring it to school tomorrow.

WILLIAM: Well, I would do. Honest I would. But my latest invention is really big. It's too big to bring into school. And anyway, it's not finished yet.

LAURA: More excuses! He's just trying to wriggle out of it!

DANNY: So what is this big invention then, William? Is it a space rocket or something? A rocket that'll fly you to Mars?

WILLIAM: *(Quietly)* Don't be silly. I couldn't make one of those in my workshop.

DANNY: *(Not listening)* Because if it's a space rocket you could fly it to school, William. Fly it to school and land on the football field!

LAURA: Anyway, your workshop's not even a proper workshop. It's just a crumbly old garden shed!

William's Workshop   Susan Gates

Where is William going when the scene opens?
Why do you think he looks "fearfully" behind him?
What is William's workshop?
Danny teases William by naming three inventions that William may or may not have tried to make. What are they?
Do you consider that Danny and Laura are bullying William? Give your reasons.
Why do you think Laura and Danny are behaving in this way?
How do you think William feels?
Do you think William is a "wimp" on the basis of the evidence in the passage?
Give the meaning of these words as they are used in the passage.
sarcastically   incredible   robot
What do you learn about Laura in this passage? Use the evidence in the passage to support what you say.
How would you like this play to end? Suggest a satisfying ending.

Writing a playscript

When you write a playscript, remember these points:

a   No inverted commas are used for speech.

b   Names of speakers are written in capital letters on the left.

c   A colon (:) separates the names of the speakers from what they say.

d   Special instructions to the actors (stage directions) are written in brackets.

Spot the differences in punctuation and layout between this conversation presented first as direct speech and then in playscript form.

Direct speech
Nervously Mrs. Jones asked, "May I come in?"
    "Of course you can, my dear," replied Mrs. White. "Come straight in and sit yourself down."
    "Oh, thank you!" said Mrs. Jones, almost in tears.

Playscript
MRS. JONES: (Nervously) May I come in?
MRS. WHITE: Of course you can, my dear. Come straight in and sit yourself down.
MRS. JONES: (Almost in tears) Oh, thank you!

A   Turn to the extract from *The Jungle Book* on page 24. Write out the conversation between Rikki-tikki and Darzee as a playscript.

B   Write a conversation between members of your family as a playscript.

C   Write one of these conversations in playscript form:

1   An argument about which television programme to watch.

2   A telephone conversation between two schoolfriends.

3   A teacher telling a pupil to work harder and a pupil protesting.

4   Two friends on a fishing trip.

D   Rewrite the last five speeches of *William's Workshop* (pages 30 and 31) as direct speech.

People

exile	A person banished from his or her native country
genius	An exceptionally brainy or gifted person
hypocrite	Pretends to be better than he or she really is
lunatic	A person who is mad
mimic	Imitates the voice and actions of others
pedestrian	Travels about on foot
prophet	Foretells coming events
traitor	Betrays his or her country, friends or any trust
tyrant	Uses his or her power to oppress others
vandal	Wilfully damages or destroys property

A Give one word for each of the following.

1 A person who attends church regularly yet leads an evil life in secret.

2 Someone who sells his or her country's secrets to a foreign power.

3 A king who treats his subjects harshly.

4 A person who is not in his or her right mind.

5 A person who has not seen his or her native land for many years.

B Complete each sentence by using a word from the list.

1 The event was foretold by a ＿＿ who lived in Israel.

2 A ＿＿ who crossed the road without looking both ways was knocked down by a car.

3 Shakespeare, who wrote some of the world's best plays, was a ＿＿ .

4 A ＿＿ had uprooted shrubs in the park and smashed several windows in the pavilion.

5 The ＿＿ gave wonderful imitations of television stars.

PEDESTRIANS ONLY

Proper adjectives

A **proper adjective** is one formed from a **proper noun**, which is the name of a particular person, place or thing.

Alps	Alpine
Belgium	Belgian
China	Chinese
Cyprus	Cypriot
Denmark	Danish
Finland	Finnish
Greece	Greek
Holland	Dutch
Iceland	Icelandic
Israel	Israeli
Malta	Maltese
Mexico	Mexican
Norway	Norwegian
Poland	Polish
Portugal	Portuguese
Spain	Spanish
Sweden	Swedish
Switzerland	Swiss
Turkey	Turkish
Venice	Venetian

A Copy these phrases, inserting in each the **proper adjective** formed from the proper noun in bold type.

1 A ＿＿ dance **Spain**
2 A ＿＿ goddess **Greece**
3 ＿＿ glass **Venice**
4 A ＿＿ restaurant **China**
5 ＿＿ bulbs **Holland**
6 ＿＿ oranges **Israel**
7 A ＿＿ cross **Malta**
8 The ＿＿ fiords **Norway**
9 An ＿＿ village **Alps**
10 ＿＿ timber **Sweden**

B Complete each sentence below by using a **proper adjective** from the list on the left.

1 Matthew is staying on a small ＿＿ island. **Greece**

2 Tampico is a ＿＿ port. **Mexico**

3 Hercule Poirot is a famous ＿＿ detective created by Agatha Christie. **Belgium**

4 ＿＿ watches are renowned for their reliability. **Switzerland**

5 A fez is a felt cap with a long tassel formerly worn by ＿＿ men. **Turkey**

6 ＿＿ wines are famous, the best known being Port Wine. **Portugal**

7 Thousands of fish were landed by the ＿＿ trawlers. **Iceland**

8 The long narrow boats used on ＿＿ canals are called gondolas. **Venice**

9 The gentian is a beautiful ＿＿ flower. **Alps**

10 The ＿＿ word "suomi" means "fish-scale". **Finland**

Nouns possession

A

To make a **singular** noun show
possession add **'s**.

Examples

the computer belonging to Mum
Mum**'s** computer

the beak of the duck
the duck**'s** beak

1   the dress belonging to Ann

2   the sword belonging to the knight

3   the thimble belonging to the tailor

4   the shop belonging to the butcher

5   the pads belonging to the cricketer

6   the jaws of the lion

7   the reward of the winner

8   the gloves of the boxer

9   the jokes of the comedian

B

To make a **plural** noun **ending
with s** show possession add **'**.

Examples

the football belonging to the boys
the boy**s'** football

the necks of the swans
the swan**s'** necks

1   the trousers belonging to the clowns

2   the tusks belonging to the elephants

3   the uniforms belonging to the sailors

4   the bones belonging to the dogs

5   the toys belonging to the girls

6   the tails of the monkeys

7   the wings of the insects

8   the nests of the birds

9   the cloakroom for ladies

C

To make a **plural** noun **which
does not end with s** show
possession, add **'s** just as with a
singular noun.

Examples

the work of the men
the men**'s** work

fashions for women
women**'s** fashions

1   handbags for women

2   the yokes belonging to the oxen

3   the tails belonging to the mice

4   the helmets belonging to the policemen

5   toys for children

6   shoes for men

7   the camp of the airmen

8   the feet of the frogmen

9   the honks of the geese

Sea-lions

Sea-lions bear some resemblance to seals, though they are much larger. When fully grown they are from twelve to twenty feet in length, and from eight to fifteen feet in circumference; they are extremely fat, so that having cut through the skin, which is about an inch in thickness, there is at least a foot of fat before you come to either lean or bones.

Their skins are covered with short grey hair, but their tails and their fins, which serve them for feet on shore, are almost black. They have a distant resemblance to an overgrown seal, though in some particulars there is a manifest difference between them, especially in the males. These have a large snout, or trunk, hanging down five or six inches below the end of the upper jaw, which the females have not.

These animals divide their time equally between the land and the sea, continuing at sea all the summer, and coming on shore at the setting in of winter, where they reside during the whole of that season. In this interval they bring forth their young, and have generally two at a birth, which they suckle with their milk, they being at first about the size of a full-grown seal. During the time these sea-lions continue on shore, they feed on the grass and small plants which grow near the banks of fresh-water streams.

They often, especially the males, have furious battles with each other, principally about their females; and we were one day surprised by the sight of two sea-lions goring each other with their teeth until they were covered with blood.

Anson's Voyage Round the World   Richard Walter

1   Which is the bigger, a sea-lion or a seal?
2   What is the length of a fully grown
    sea-lion?
3   What is the thickness of a sea-lion's skin?
4   What thickness of fat lies between the skin of a
    sea-lion and its flesh or bones?
5   What purpose is served by the sea-lion's tail and fins
    when it is on shore?
6   Where does the sea-lion spend the summer?
7   Where does it spend the winter?
8   At what time of year are young sea-lions born?
9   How does the face of a male sea-lion differ from that
    of a female?
10 What do the male sea-lions fight about, chiefly?

Contractions

Can't is a short way of writing **cannot**.

I'll is a short way of writing **I will**.

These shortened forms are called **contractions**. Now see how the word **would** is used in contractions.

I would	I'd
she would	she'd
you would	you'd
we would	we'd
he would	he'd
they would	they'd

you would

you **would**

you'd

A   In each sentence write a contraction in place of the words in bold type.

1   The police said **they would** be glad of the information.

2   Our teacher asked us if **we would** like to have a concert.

3   I think **you would** be interested in this book.

4   Dad said **he would** give me a football next week.

5   Mum promised **she would** help me to swim.

6   The doctor told me **I would** be better in a few days.

B   Write the contractions for the following.

1	I am	11	have not
2	you have	12	she will
3	she is	13	I would
4	will not	14	we are
5	he would	15	are not
6	do not	16	you are
7	they are	17	we would
8	shall not	18	they have
9	we have	19	cannot
10	it is	20	they will

C   Write the words for which the contractions stand.

1   I **can't** forget that **I'm** bereft
Of all the pleasant sights they see.
The Pied Piper of Hamelin

2   Said Francis then, "Faith, gentlemen, **we're** better here than there."
The Glove and the Lions

3   The old sage said, "**You're** as sound as a nut."
The Enchanted Shirt

4   Out spoke a wife: "**We've** beds at home;
We'll burn them for a light?"
The Wives of Brixham

Antonyms opposites

absent	present
admit	deny
advance	retreat
arrival	departure
bold	timid
cheap	expensive
conceal	reveal
danger	safety
failure	success
false	true
hollow	solid
hurry	loiter
ignorance	knowledge
innocent	guilty
joy	sorrow
miser	spendthrift
permit	forbid
plentiful	scarce
poverty	wealth
proud	humble
seldom	often
shallow	deep
superior	inferior
wild	tame
win	lose

A Write the **opposites** of the following words.

1	joy	7	guilty	13	false
2	miser	8	advance	14	plentiful
3	cheap	9	hollow	15	failure
4	admit	10	arrival	16	poverty
5	permit	11	bold	17	hurry
6	ignorance	12	proud	18	conceal

B Complete each sentence by inserting the **opposite** of the word in bold type.

1 Mum's new coat was quite **cheap**, but her shoes were very ____ .

2 Nine members were **present** and three were ____ .

3 Some of the defendant's statements were **true**, but many were ____ .

4 Megan dived in at the **deep** end; Kayleigh paddled at the ____ end.

5 Sally always **hurries** home from school but Carol often ____ on the way.

6 Kevin is **innocent** but everyone knows that his brother is ____ .

C In each column find the **two antonyms** or opposites. Use your dictionary to help you.

1	2	3
curious	plentiful	attack
violent	superior	forbid
guilty	scarce	receive
innocent	brilliant	permit

4	5	6
timid	happiness	unknown
simple	poverty	heavy
huge	thrift	famous
bold	wealth	popular

7	8	9
bright	stop	acquire
apathetic	forget	sell
light	pay	purchase
enthusiastic	start	gamble

reveal

conceal

Direct and indirect speech

Direct speech

"Have you cleaned your teeth, Nigel?" asked his mother.

The sentence contains the **exact words** spoken by Nigel's mother.

Direct speech always requires inverted commas, or speech marks, " ".

Indirect speech

Nigel's mother asked him if he had cleaned his teeth.

This sentence does not contain the exact words spoken by Nigel's mother.

Indirect speech does not require inverted commas.

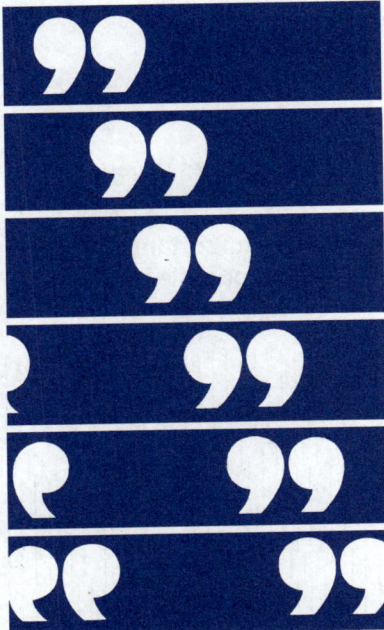

A   Change to **indirect speech**.

1   "Can I have a bicycle for my birthday?" asked Matthew.

2   "I have a bad headache, so I think I will lie down," said Mr. Dean.

3   "The days are certainly getting longer," remarked Mr. Caldwell.

4   "Do you know how to play darts, Roger?" asked David.

5   "You look as if you could do with a good holiday," said Mrs. Smith to her son.

6   "Peter, tuck your shirt in!" ordered his mother.

7   "Come inside, Mrs. Dale," invited the old lady, "and have tea with us."

B   Change to **direct speech**.

1   The shoe repairer told Robert that his shoes would be ready by Saturday.

2   Simon's mother asked him if he had loitered on the way home from school.

3   Bernard's teacher asked him if he had ever spent a holiday in France.

4   Bernard replied that he had once been on a day trip to Dieppe.

5   The headmaster told the boys that their work was improving.

6   Judith told her father that she had come top in English.

7   Her father promised to give her ten pounds if she stopped biting her nails for three months.

8   My mother said that she was feeling tired.

9   I said that I should love to come.

10   The doctor advised me to stay home from school.

Opposites using a prefix

The opposites of some words can be formed by writing before them **un**, **in**, **il**, **dis**, **ir** or **im**.

un
aware
certain
favourable
fortunate
grateful
important
kind
necessary
popular
usual

dis
appear
approve
connect
continue
courteous
honest
obedient
orderly
regard
similar

in
considerate
efficient
equality
frequent
gratitude
human
sane

ir
regular
responsible
reverent

il
legal

im
movable
patient
perfect
probable
proper

A Form the opposites of these words, using prefixes.

1	sane	9	certain
2	aware	10	perfect
3	human	11	gratitude
4	usual	12	regard
5	obedient	13	continue
6	approve	14	considerate
7	equality	15	orderly
8	similar		

B Select a word from the list to complete each sentence.

1 An ____ event is one which will probably never happen.

2 An object which cannot be moved is ____ .

3 An ____ person gives no thanks for kindnesses received.

4 Another word for ____ is unlawful.

5 An ____ person is not responsible for his actions.

6 An ____ article is one you can do without.

7 The word ____ means unlucky.

8 A ____ person is rude and ill-mannered.

C Use these phrases in sentences of your own, but give the word in bold type an opposite meaning.

1 a **popular** man   4 an **important** town
2 **regular** attendance   5 **favourable** weather
3 an **efficient** worker 6 a **proper** remark

dis

Diminutives

A diminutive is a word representing something small or something young.

Examples

kitten
a young cat

booklet
a small book

bear	cub
cod	codling
deer	fawn
dog	puppy
eagle	eaglet
eel	elver
elephant	calf
frog	tadpole
goose	gosling
hare	leveret
horse	foal
mare	filly
owl	owlet
river	rivulet
sheep	lamb
stream	streamlet
swan	cygnet
trout	fry
whale	calf

A   Write one word for each of the following:

1	a young eel	10	a young cod
2	a baby goose	11	a baby frog
3	a young elephant	12	a young deer
4	a young sheep	13	a young whale
5	a young hare	14	a small river
6	a small stream	15	a young mare
7	a baby owl	16	a young bear
8	a young horse	17	a baby eagle
9	a young dog	18	a young swan

B   Write the words which are missing from these sentences.

1   Several tiny _____ followed the eel up the river.

2   The mare and her _____ trotted round the paddock.

3   The _____ and her leverets lay down in the long grass.

4   The _____ and the foal were sold for £900.

5   The _____ and her lamb grazed in the field.

6   The elephant and her _____ walked slowly into the jungle clearing.

7   A swan and her two _____ floated majestically downstream.

8   The cat carried her _____ in her mouth.

The Royal Mint

Hundreds of years ago coins were made in various towns in Britain, including Bristol, Canterbury, London, Winchester and York. After 1810 there was only one Royal Mint, that on Tower Hill, London, but in 1968 a new mint was established at Llantrisant, South Wales, for the manufacture of Britain's decimal currency which was introduced on 15th February 1971.

The metal ingots from which coins are made are melted in closed crucibles for about two hours, and the molten metal is then run into moulds to form coinage-bars which vary in width and thickness according to the coins that are to be made. These bars or strips are next passed between rollers to ensure that they are of uniform size and then put into machines which punch out the blank discs on which the design is to be stamped. After being examined to see that they are of the correct size and shape, these blank discs are fed into annealing drums which soften the metal in preparation for the stamping process. The design is stamped by powerful presses, both sides being done at the same time, and the finished coins are placed on a moving belt for inspection by overlookers who are trained to detect any faults. The newly-minted coins are tested for weight and, after being counted by an automatic machine, are placed in bags, sealed and stored in large strongrooms until required by the banks.

There are no silver coins in Britain's decimal currency, cupronickel being used for the 50p, 10p and 5p pieces.

A sealed bag of 50p pieces contains £250 worth, or 500 coins. Each bag of 10p pieces and 5p pieces contains £100 worth.

1   Name three towns at which coins were made hundreds of years ago.
2   After 1810 there was only one Royal Mint. Where was that?
3   Where was a new Royal Mint established in 1968?
4   When was Britain's decimal currency introduced?
5   How are metal ingots made into coinage-bars?
6   Why are these bars passed between rollers?
7   Why are the blank discs fed into annealing drums?
8   How are the finished coins counted?
9   What metal is used in place of silver for the decimal coins?
10 How many coins would there be in a bag of 5p pieces?

£100
10p

£250
50p

Using the right pronoun

Mistakes are often made in the use of the pronouns **I** and **me**.

Which is correct?

Dad and **me** are going to the football match *or* Dad and **I** are going to the football match.

Make two sentences.

a Dad is going to the football match.
b **I** am going to the football match.

Me am going to the football match would be wrong.

So the correct sentence is

Dad and **I** are going to the football match.

Which is correct?

Uncle George sent a ticket for Dad and **me** *or* Uncle George sent a ticket for Dad and **I**.

Make two sentences.

a Uncle George sent a ticket for Dad.
b Uncle George sent a ticket for **me**.

Uncle George sent a ticket for **I** would be wrong.

So the correct sentence is

Uncle George sent a ticket for Dad and **me**.

After the word **between** always use the pronoun **me**.

Examples
Between you and **I** he can't afford a new car. (*wrong*)
Between you and **me** he can't afford a new car. (*right*)

Insert **I** or **me** to complete each sentence.

1 Pavana and ____ have won prizes in the drawing competition.

2 Prizes have been awarded to Pavana and ____ .

3 Beth and ____ have been invited to Amy's party.

4 Amy has invited Beth and ____ to her party.

5 This is a secret between you and ____ .

6 You and ____ must keep this matter secret.

7 The headmaster punished Ossie and ____ for being so late.

8 Ossie and ____ were punished by the headmaster for being so late.

9 Leroy and ____ are to share the sweets between us.

10 These sweets are to be shared between Leroy and ____ .

Alphabetical order

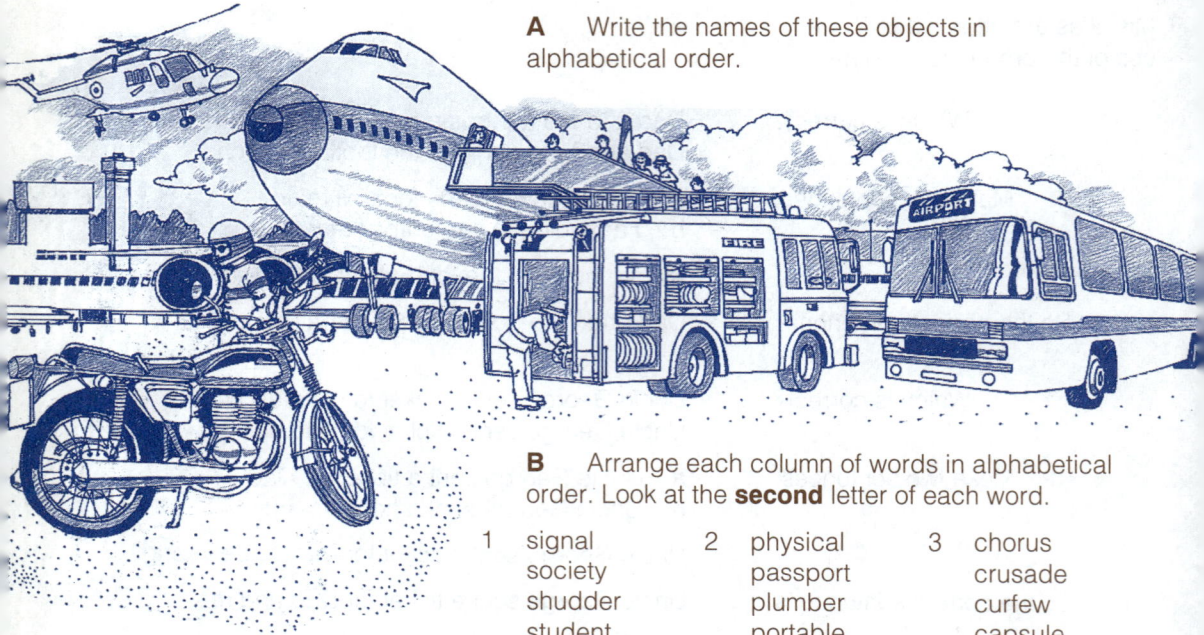

A   Write the names of these objects in alphabetical order.

B   Arrange each column of words in alphabetical order. Look at the **second** letter of each word.

1	signal	2	physical	3	chorus
	society		passport		crusade
	shudder		plumber		curfew
	student		portable		capsule
	skier		peculiar		climate

C   Look at the **third** letter of each word when arranging them in alphabetical order.

1	blizzard	2	ground	3	splint
	blunder		granite		sparrow
	blockade		gruesome		sprawl
	bladder		grease		spectre
	bleak		gristle		spiral

Look at these words:
hear; **hea**p; **hea**t; **hea**d; **hea**l

Notice that the **first three letters** of each word are the same – **hea**.

To arrange these words in alphabetical order, we must look at the **fourth** letter of each.

These are:
r p t d l

Letters in alphabetical order:
d l p r t

Words in alphabetical order:
hea**d**   hea**l**   hea**p**   hea**r**   hea**t**

D   Arrange in alphabetical order, looking at the **fourth** letter.

1	catkin	2	promise	3	sprout
	cattle		profit		spruce
	catch		produce		sprint
	catalogue		problem		spray
	catgut		proceed		spread
4	retreat	5	patriot	6	assume
	return		patch		assist
	retail		pattern		assets
	retort		patent		assault
	retire		patient		assorted

Adjectives formation

Many adjectives are formed by adding **-ous** to a word.

Examples

danger**ous**   prosper**ous**
pomp**ous**   riot**ous**

Sometimes spelling changes are made when **-ous** is added.

1 Drop final **e**.
famous   porous
ridiculous   continuous

2 Change **y** to **i**.
furious   injurious
envious

3 Double the last letter.
marvellous   libellous

4 Drop a letter.
humorous   vigorous
glamorous

5 Other changes.
cautious   grievous
miraculous

Atropa Belladonna

POISONOUS

A   Write the missing **adjectives**. When in difficulty consult your dictionary.

1 A substance which is full of pores is ____ .

2 A person who has won fame is ____ .

3 A person who envies others is ____ .

4 A game which is played with vigour is ____ .

5 A room in which there is plenty of space is ____ .

6 A business which prospers is ____ .

7 Berries which poison are ____ .

8 An adventure in which there is peril is ____ .

9 A person who behaves like a villain is ____ .

10 A person who eats like a glutton is ____ .

B   Complete each sentence by using the **adjective** formed from the word in bold type.

1 *The Adventures of Tom Sawyer* is a ____ story. **humour**

2 The travellers gazed at the ____ scenery. **marvel**

3 The millionaire lives in a ____ house in France. **luxury**

4 The history of Britain is studded with ____ deeds. **glory**

5 When he heard of the retreat the general was ____ . **fury**

6 Paul has always been a ____ boy. **mischief**

7 Hosepipes were turned on the ____ crowd. **riot**

8 The show is ____ from 5.30 to 11 p.m. **continue**

9 Dense fog and smoke are ____ to health. **injury**

10 The crew of the trawler had a ____ escape from death. **miracle**

Joining sentences

You have learned in Book 3 how to join sentences by using **conjunctions**.

You can also join sentences by using **who**, **whom**, **that** and **which** (**relative pronouns**) and **whose** (**relative adjective**).

Examples

This is the lady.
She found your kitten.
This is the lady **who** found your kitten.

That is the man.
I saw him yesterday.
That is the man **whom** I saw yesterday.

These are the trainers.
I like them best.
These are the trainers **which** I like best.
These are the trainers **that** I like best.

The policeman spoke to the woman.
Her wallet had been stolen.
The policeman spoke to the woman **whose** wallet had been stolen.

A   Use **who**, **whom**, **that**, **which** or **whose** to join each pair of sentences.

1   The police arrested the youth.
He had robbed the bank.

2   Mrs. Baird gave Angela a bracelet.
It was made of gold.

3   The door was opened by a young girl.
She looked very unhappy.

4   This is the house.
Jack built it.

5   Sitting near us was a woman.
Her hair had been dyed blue.

B   Use **who**, **whom**, **that**, **which** or **whose** to fill the gaps in these sentences.

1   Do you know anybody ____ first name beings with H?

2   Colin was the only pupil ____ was willing to help tidy up.

3   The prize ____ everyone wanted to win was the trip in a hot air balloon.

4   Anna is a friend ____ I have known all my life.

5   The canoe ____ was painted bright yellow was soon spotted by the helicopter crew.

C   Complete the sentences below.

1   . . . . whose dog escaped . . . .

2   . . . . that Dad bought . . . .

3   . . . . which you caught yesterday . . . .

4   . . . . whom I like very much.

5   . . . . who helped me . . . .

Similes

When something is very **heavy** we say it is **as heavy as lead**.

This is because it is similar to lead in **weight**, although it may be quite different in other ways.

An expression of this kind is called a **simile**.

as sweet as sugar
as bold as brass
as brave as a lion
as bright as a button
as busy as a bee
as clean as a new pin
as cool as a cucumber
as dead as a doornail
as deaf as a doorpost
as fit as a fiddle

A Write the missing words.

1 The old man was as ＿＿ as a doorpost.

2 In walked James as ＿＿ as brass.

3 Old Jacob Marley was as ＿＿ as a doornail.

4 After a hot bath he was as ＿＿ as a new pin.

5 Ann was as busy as a ＿＿ , helping Dad in the garden.

6 The full-back was as cool as a ＿＿ .

7 Every player in the team was as fit as a ＿＿ .

8 David got up at seven o'clock as bright as a ＿＿ .

When using similes, it is always best to use your own fresh, original ones.

This is one that a pupil made up:
The twigs were stretched out **like a skinny hand**.

B Complete these descriptions as vividly as you can.

1 James opened his exercise book with a heart as heavy as ＿＿ .

2 Sarah limped along the road like ＿＿ .

3 The princess's eyes were as blue as ＿＿ .

4 The ogre's breath smelt just like ＿＿ .

5 The headmaster's angry voice cut through the laughter like ＿＿ .

C Look again at the comparisons you have supplied in exercise **B** and explain why you think the similes are effective.

Inside the vault

James sat down on the steps of the tomb and watched. The light ebbed from the church. Shadows began to pack the roof and crowd around the pillars and dark oak pews. The knight and his lady lay on their tomb with worn faces and stiff stone drapery. He was a crusading knight, armoured from head to pointed feet, his hands frozen in prayer; he must have known strange, hot, far-away places, and then come back to die in Ledsham, among elms and willows beside the Evenlode. James fetched himself a hassock to sit on that had been embroidered by the ladies of Ledsham Women's Institute, and thought about this, and other things, and listened to the tapping noises of Bert's pick and watched the dust and chippings fly up around the flagstone.

"I think this is the one," said Bert. "I reckon it is."

"What if someone comes?" said James.

"I'm seeing about the damp, aren't I?" said Bert. "Rising damp, they've got here. I don't know anything about any vault."

The church was very dark and quiet now, but not empty because no place that has been used for so long by so many people can ever be empty. Like all old buildings, it was full of their thoughts and feelings, and these thoughts and feelings seemed to crowd in upon James as he sat waiting and watching. He had asked Arnold to come, and Arnold had come at once and was there now, at James' elbow, waiting and watching with him.

"Here she comes," said Bert. He put his pick down and dug his fingers down under the edge of the flagstone. He heaved, muscles stood out like cords in his arms, the flagstone rocked, and tipped on to one side. James leaned forward.

"Hang on," said Bert, "I got to get through the next bit. I told you I mortared it up again." He swung the pick down: the floor split, mortar crumbled away downwards, and there was a jagged black hole, man-sized.

"There we are," said Bert. "Let's have that torch."

He pointed the torch down into the hole. "Want to have a look?"

James clutched the edge of the stone step. He said to Arnold, "Shall I?" and Arnold told him he'd be a silly idiot not to. He got up, rather slowly, and came forward, and lay down on his stomach and shone the torch down into the hole.

It was smaller than he'd expected. A little, crumbling underground room, with rough masonry walls and rubble all over the floor. And long stone boxes stacked up on top of each other: several at one side, one by itself on the other.

Bert's face appeared at the other side of the hole. "Let's have some light over here."

James swung the torch around. They could see the lettering now on top of the solitary box, black-shadowed in the beam of light. "I thought so," said Bert.

**Here lyeth ye body of
Thomas Kempe Apothecarie
he departed this life ye last of October AD 1629
in the 63 yeare of his Age.**

"Apothecary?" said James. His voice dropped into the vault, sounding deep and hollow.

"He couldn't go having them put sorcerer, could he?" said Bert. "Not if he wanted to be in here. The Church wouldn't hold with that."

"Why do you think he wanted to be there?" said James in a whisper. "He wasn't very religious, was he? Believing in all that magic, and hating priests."

The Ghost of Thomas Kempe   Penelope Lively

1 Why are Bert, Arnold and James in the church?
2 What will Bert pretend he is doing if anyone else comes in?
3 Why are the faces of the knight and his lady described as **worn**?
4 In what way are the knight's hands **frozen** in prayer?
5 What is a **hassock**?
6 How does Bert know that the flagstone he is trying to lift has been mortared in place?
7 Who is the first of the three to look into the vault?
8 Why is the small room very dark?
9 What are the long stone boxes?
10 On which side of the room is Thomas Kempe's box?
11 Give the day and month of Thomas Kempe's death.
12 In what century did Thomas Kempe die?
13 How old was he when he died?
14 What was his occupation as indicated on the box?
15 What was his true occupation?
16 Why could Thomas Kempe not have his true occupation shown on the box?
17 Say in what two ways he was not a religious man.

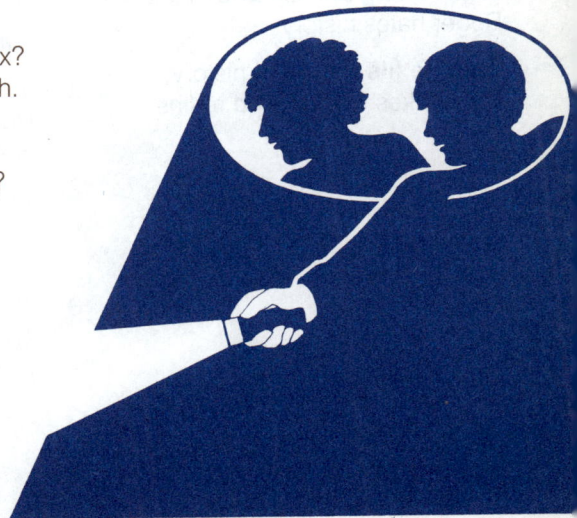

Joining sentences

You have already practised joining two sentences with conjunctions and relative pronouns.

It is possible to join together more than two sentences, and you can experiment with joining them in lots of different ways.

Example

Roger likes English.
He likes maths.
He hates history.

Roger likes English **and** maths **but** hates history.

Roger hates history **but** he likes English **and** maths.

Although Roger hates history, he likes English **and** maths.

Roger, **who** likes English **and** maths, hates history.

Roger, **who** hates history, likes English **and** maths.

While liking English **and** maths, Roger hates history.

Despite his hatred of history, Roger likes English **and** maths.

A Write one sentence in place of each group below.

1 The day was cold.
The day was windy.
It was only the first day of February.

2 The dog was barking.
He was trying to get over the gate.
The children kept away from him.

3 The office had closed.
The staff had departed.
It was not yet five o'clock.

4 I had intended to go for a walk.
It started to snow.
I sat by the fire.
I fell fast asleep.

5 Andrew had a bad leg.
He was unable to walk.
He stayed indoors with Gillian.
She read several stories to him.

6 We set off for the woods.
After a while there was a thunderstorm.
We had to shelter in an old barn.
It was close at hand.

B Combine each group of sentences below in two different ways.

1 Jake was frightened.
He was a nervous child.
His mother was late.

2 Work steadily.
Learn from your mistakes.
You will make progress.

3 The kitten was black.
The kitten was thin.
It was very hungry.
It had been abandoned.

Using the right verb

Learn how these verbs are used, then answer the questions.

to **accede** to a **request**
to **avert** a **catastrophe**
to **contract** a **disease**
to **contradict** a **statement**
to **denounce** an **impostor**
to **disperse** a **mob**
to **estimate** the **cost**
to **evade capture**
to **exterminate pests**
to **impart knowledge**
to **impose** a **fine**
to **inflict punishment**
to **inherit** a **fortune**
to **interpret** a **foreign language**
to **liberate** a **prisoner**
to **prophesy** the **future**
to **redeem** a **promise**
to **reveal** a **secret**
to **surmount** an **obstacle**
to **trespass** on **another's land**

A   Copy and complete these phrases.

1   to ____ a secret
2   to ____ punishment
3   to ____ capture
4   to ____ knowledge
5   to ____ an obstacle
6   to ____ a prisoner
7   to ____ an impostor
8   to ____ the cost
9   to ____ a disease
10 to ____ on another's land
11 to interpret a ____
12 to inherit a ____
13 to disperse a ____
14 to accede to a ____
15 to prophesy the ____
16 to redeem a ____
17 to exterminate ____
18 to avert a ____
19 to contradict a ____
20 to impose a ____

B   Write the verb which will complete each sentence correctly. Use the past tense where required.

1   On his father's death he will ____ a million pounds.

2   The magistrates ____ a fine of £50 and costs.

3   Mounted police were brought in to ____ the demonstrators.

4   The girl who ____ leukaemia is seriously ill.

5   A teacher should not only possess knowledge; he or she should know how to ____ it.

6   Simon ____ a dreadful accident by warning the police there was an obstacle on the railway track.

7   For nearly a month the escaped convict ____ capture.

8   The cost of building the new school is ____ at £6,000,000.

Idioms

In Book 3 you learnt ten sayings which are in common use.

Example to get into hot water means to get into trouble

Expressions of this kind are called **idioms**.

Idiom	Meaning
to have an axe to grind	to have something to gain by an action
to be a wet blanket	to be a spoilsport
to draw the long bow	to exaggerate
to make a clean breast of it	to confess to some wrong
to take the bull by the horns	to meet difficulties boldly
to be under a cloud	to be under suspicion
to be a dog in a manger	to deny to others what is useless to oneself
to show the white feather	to show cowardice
to bury the hatchet	to settle a quarrel and live in peace
to flog a dead horse	to do work which produces no results

A Complete these **idioms** and describe a situation where each could apply.

1 to be under a ___
2 to flog a ___ horse
3 to be a dog in a ___
4 to draw the ___ ___
5 to bury the ___
6 to have an axe ___ ___
7 to take the bull ___ ___ ___
8 to be a wet ___
9 to make a clean ___ ___ ___
10 to show the white ___

B Rewrite these sentences, substituting the **idiom** for the words in bold type.

1 The detective was determined to **meet the difficulties boldly**.

2 Jamie told his uncle not to be a **spoilsport**.

3 The old rivals will soon **settle their quarrel and live in peace**.

4 The prefect was **under suspicion** at school.

5 The old sailor is very fond of **exaggerating**.

Synonyms similars

abrupt	sudden
accommodation	room
altitude	height
amiable	friendly
brief	short
comprehend	understand
demonstrate	show
diminutive	small
disperse	scatter
eminent	famous
endeavour	try
interior	inside
intoxicated	drunk
invincible	unbeatable
loathe	hate
melancholy	sad
odour	smell
penetrate	pierce
prohibited	forbidden
reluctant	unwilling

A   Write a simpler word in place of each word in bold type.

1   Smoking in the factory is **prohibited**.

2   The **odour** of fried sausages came from the kitchen.

3   I read a **brief** report of the accident.

4   We failed to obtain **accommodation** at the hotel.

5   This year our cricket team has proved **invincible**.

6   He was most **reluctant** to leave home.

7   We will **endeavour** to deliver the goods today.

8   Mounted police were sent to **disperse** the large crowd.

9   The plane was flying at an **altitude** of 10,000 metres.

10   Our train came to an **abrupt** stop.

B   In each group below select the word which is similar in meaning to the word in bold type.

1   **eminent**

handsome
skilful
famous

2   **intoxicated**

drunk
unconscious
sober

3   **comprehend**

fear
understand
pretend

4   **loathe**

hate
adore
respect

5   **demonstrate**

fight
squander
show

6   **interior**

cheap
inside
common

7   **amiable**

rude
stout
friendly

8   **melancholy**

sad
jolly
greedy

9   **penetrate**

thicken
pierce
collapse

10   **diminutive**

tough
dark
small

11   **abrupt**

sudden
brief
rough

12   **odour**

dislike
heavy
smell

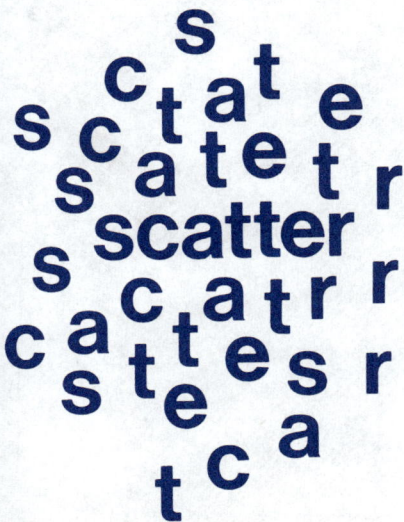

53

A pony for Jody

Jody could begin to see things now. He looked into the box stall and then stepped back quickly.

A red pony colt was looking at him out of the stall. Its tense ears were forward and a light of disobedience was in its eyes. Its coat was rough and thick as an Airedale's fur and its mane was long and tangled. Jody's throat collapsed in on itself and cut his breath short.

"He needs a good currying," his father said, "and if I ever hear of you not feeding him or leaving his stall dirty I'll sell him off in a minute."

Jody couldn't bear to look at the pony's eyes any more. He gazed down at his hands for a moment, and he asked very shyly: "Mine?" No one answered him. He put his hand out toward the pony. Its grey nose came close, sniffing loudly, and then the lips drew back and the strong teeth closed on Jody's fingers. The pony shook its head up and down and seemed to laugh with amusement. Jody regarded his bruised fingers. "Well," he said with pride – "well, I guess he can bite all right." The two men laughed, somewhat in relief. Carl Tiflin went out of the barn and walked up a side-hill to be by himself, for he was embarrassed, but Billy Buck stayed. It was easier to talk to Billy Buck. Jody asked again – "Mine?"

Billy became professional in tone. "Sure! That is, if you look out for him and break him right. I'll show you how. He's just a colt. You can't ride him for some time."

The Red Pony   John Steinbeck

1   Why did Jody step back from the box stall?
2   Which two words indicate the pony's mood and attitude?
3   Why did Jody's throat "collapse in on itself"?
4   What is another word for **currying**?
5   What two things did Jody's father warn him he must do?
6   Why couldn't he bear to look at the pony's eyes any more?
7   How did Jody bruise his fingers?
8   Why did Jody speak of the pony with pride?
9   Why were the two men relieved as they laughed?
10 Why did Carl Tiflin want to be by himself?
11 Why could the pony not be ridden for some time?
12 Who was going to help Jody break in the pony?

Silent letters

Some words can be difficult to spell because they contain silent letters.

Learn the words in these lists and then answer the questions in exercise A.

silent c
ascend
crescent
muscle
scenery
scent
science
scissors

silent p
cupboard
pneumatic
pneumonia
psalm
psychology
raspberry
receipt

silent h
exhausted
ghost
honest
rhubarb
rhyme
shepherd
vehicle

silent t
castle
christen
fasten
listen
mistletoe
moisten
whistle

A   Fill each space with the missing silent letter. Refer to the lists on the left.

1   tired out
ex _ austed

2   a curving road
cres _ ent

3   a sacred song
_ salm

4   to make slightly damp
mois _ en

5   a person who looks after sheep
shep _ erd

6   inflammation of the lungs
_ neumonia

B   Use your dictionary to help you find these words.

1   an extinct winged reptile
pte _ _ _ _ _ _ _

2   mixed; of all sorts
mis _ _ _ _ _ _ _ _ _

3   sum of money borrowed to buy a house
mor _ _ _ _ _

4   colour of army uniforms
kha _ _

5   a pen-name; assumed name
pse _ _ _ _ _ _

6   amazed and horrified
agh _ _ _

7   person entitled to inherit
he _ _

8   small boat
din _ _ _

9   an evergreen shrub with large flowers
rho _ _ _ _ _ _ _ _

10   a bird of the grouse family
pta _ _ _ _ _ _

Sentence structure

Let me know when you are ready.

When you are ready let me know.

Both these sentences contain exactly the same words, although not in the same order.

a A rattlesnake **bit** the lumberjack.

b The lumberjack **was bitten** by a rattlesnake.

Both these sentences convey the same idea, but the words they contain are not exactly the same.

(a) contains the word **bit**, the **past tense** of bite.

(b) contains the word **bitten**, the **past participle** of bite.

A Rewrite each sentence below, using the same words, but commencing with the word in bold type.

1 Julia persisted in talking **although** she had been warned not to do so.

2 She ordered the dress **without** thinking how she could pay for it.

3 Two sailors were having an argument **on** the quay.

4 The convict was recaptured **just** as night was falling.

5 The express train rushed into the tunnel **with** a shriek of its whistle.

6 You will be seriously ill **if** you do not check that cough.

7 A huge log fire blazed **in** the great hall of the castle.

8 The girl was up and about **long** before daybreak.

B Rewrite these sentences, beginning with the word in bold type in each case, and making such changes as are necessary.

1 Charles Dickens wrote **A** Christmas Carol.

2 The Rovers beat **the** Wanderers 2-0 last Saturday.

3 A gang of thieves stole **the** valuable portrait.

4 The County Architect drew **the** plans of the dining-hall.

5 The heavy fall shook **the** frail old gentleman.

6 The twins took **Spot** to the park.

7 Our puppy tore **that** curtain.

8 The three girls chose **the** curtains for the lounge.

9 The one-eyed parrot had eaten **every** single chocolate.

10 Penelope Lively wrote **The** Ghost of Thomas Kempe.

Alphabetical order

A Arrange the words in each group in alphabetical order. Look at the **fifth** letter of each word.

1	straw	2	handicap	3	catapult
	strap		handy		catastrophe
	straight		handsome		catalogue
	stray		handle		catacomb
	strand		handful		cataract

4	fortress	5	partner	6	compile
	fortunate		partly		complain
	fortify		partake		compel
	forth		party		compose
	fortnight		partial		compare

This is a drawing of a ten-volume encyclopaedia. Each volume is numbered and also shows the first four letters of the first word and the last word it contains.

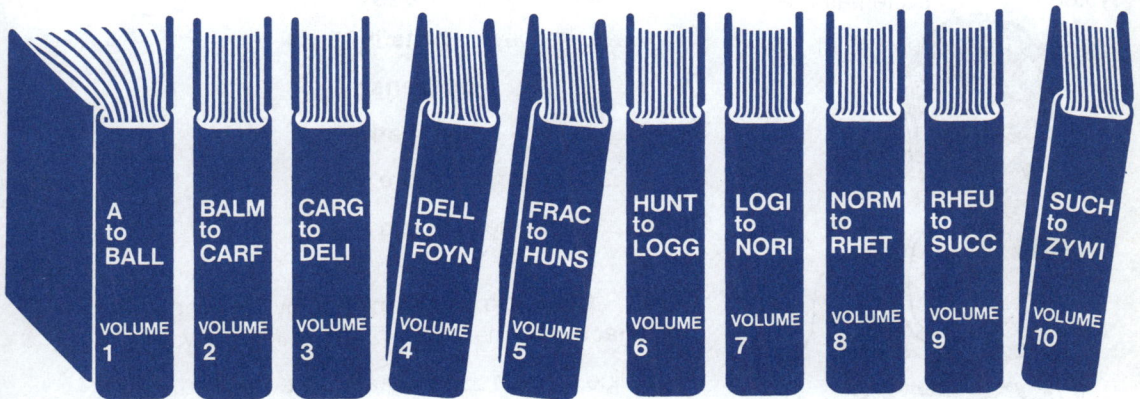

A to BALL	BALM to CARF	CARG to DELI	DELL to FOYN	FRAC to HUNS	HUNT to LOGG	LOGI to NORI	NORM to RHET	RHEU to SUCC	SUCH to ZYWI
VOLUME 1	VOLUME 2	VOLUME 3	VOLUME 4	VOLUME 5	VOLUME 6	VOLUME 7	VOLUME 8	VOLUME 9	VOLUME 10

B Give the numbers of the volumes in which you would look for the following words.

1	longitude	8	athletics	15	foundry
2	Dunlop	9	portcullis	16	decimal
3	meteor	10	Henry VIII	17	resin
4	indigo	11	Kiel Canal	18	Napoleon
5	cardinal	12	gannet	19	shorthand
6	balsa	13	vodka	20	crypt
7	tambourine	14	Jolly Roger		

Adjectives formation

Noun	Adjective
athlete	athletic
benefit	beneficial
circle	circular
credit	creditable
custom	customary
effect	effective
energy	energetic
fire	fiery
fraud	fraudulent
giant	gigantic
influence	influential
metal	metallic
method	methodical
muscle	muscular
nonsense	nonsensical
picture	picturesque
science	scientific
skill	skilful
sympathy	sympathetic
system	systematic

A   Form **adjectives** from these nouns.

1	muscle	7	skill	13	science
2	effect	8	benefit	14	fire
3	fraud	9	system	15	picture
4	athlete	10	credit	16	influence
5	sympathy	11	method	17	circle
6	energy	12	giant	18	metal

B   Write the missing **adjectives**.

1   an ___ remedy   **effect**

2   a ___ craftsman   **skill**

3   a ___ sound   **metal**

4   an ___ man   **athlete**

5   a ___ age   **science**

6   a ___ saw   **circle**

7   an ___ worker   **energy**

8   a ___ holiday   **benefit**

9   a ___ reply   **nonsense**

10   a ___ friend   **sympathy**

11   a ___ scene   **picture**

12   a ___ scheme   **fraud**

C   Complete each sentence by inserting the **adjective** formed from the noun in bold type.

1   Police made a ___ search of the building.
system

2   The scientist is noted for his ___ work.   **method**

3   Paul's success was a most ___ achievement.
credit

4   The key was not in its ___ place.   **custom**

5   We stayed at a ___ Cornish fishing village.
picture

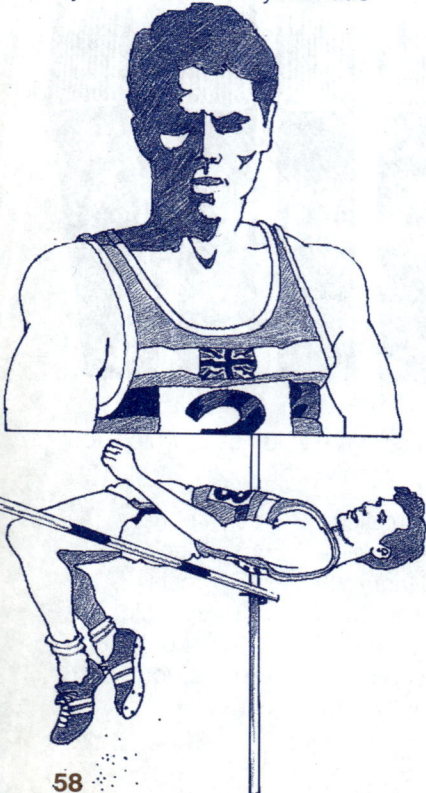

Capital letters

Capital letters are used for:

names of persons

pets

days

months *but not seasons*

special holidays

geographical names

nations

languages

titles of books, poems, songs, etc.

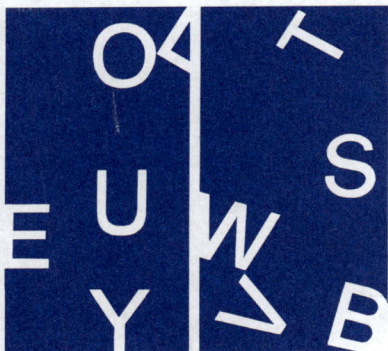

A Rewrite these sentences, using capital letters where necessary.

1 the river thames is sometimes referred to as old father thames.

2 both german and italian are taught at grosvenor grammar school.

3 rudyard kipling, who was born in india, wrote many fine books, the most famous being the jungle book.

4 easter is a movable festival which may come in march or april, but christmas is not.

5 the bank of england is sometimes called the old lady of threadneedle street.

6 linda's brother colin is a patient at the middlesex hospital.

7 the white tower in the tower of london was built by gundulf, bishop of rochester, about A.D. 1078.

8 from monday to friday the shop closes at 5.30; on saturdays it closes at 1 o'clock.

B Some punctuation marks are missing from the sentences below. Write out the sentences correctly punctuated.

1 Would you like to tour Europe and see its wonderful sights

2 In the market there were ample supplies of apples pears oranges bananas peaches and grapes

3 James did you give my message to the headmaster asked his mother

4 Yes Mum I gave it to him before lessons began replied James

5 Some members wont be present but it doesnt matter

6 The ticket bore the date Thurs 26th Sept in bold type

7 The bat we played with was Toms but the ball was Duncans

8 Oh dear exclaimed Miss Taylor in alarm I have lost my purse

Encounter with a dinosaur

Something was swimming toward the lighthouse tower.

It was a cold night, as I have said; the high tower was cold, the light coming and going and the Fog Horn calling and calling through the ravelling mist. You couldn't see far and you couldn't see plain, but there was the deep sea moving on its way about the night earth, flat and quiet, the colour of grey mud, and here were the two of us alone in the high tower, and there, far out at first, was a ripple, followed by a wave, a rising, a bubble, a bit of froth. And then, from the surface of the cold sea came a head, a large head, dark-coloured, with immense eyes, and then a neck. And then – not a body – but more neck and more! The head rose a full forty feet above the water on a slender and beautiful dark neck. Only then did the body, like a little island of black coral and shells and crayfish, drip up from the subterranean. There was a flicker of tail. In all, from head to tail, I estimated the monster at ninety or a hundred feet.

I don't know what I said. I said something.

"Steady, boy, steady," whispered McDunn.

"It's impossible!" I said.

"No, Johnny, *we're* impossible. *It's* like it always was ten million years ago. It hasn't changed. It's *us* and the land that've changed, become impossible. *Us!*"

It swam slowly and with a great dark majesty out in the icy waters, far away. The fog came and went about it, momentarily erasing its shape.

The Fog Horn   Ray Bradbury

1   Where were the men standing?
2   What sound could be heard?
3   How much visibility was there?
4   Which movement first told the men there was something in the sea?
5   Where did the men first see this movement?
6   At what height above the water did the head rise?
7   To what does the writer compare the monster's body?
8   How long was the monster?
9   When did McDunn suggest these monsters had once lived?
10   Why was the monster not continuously visible?

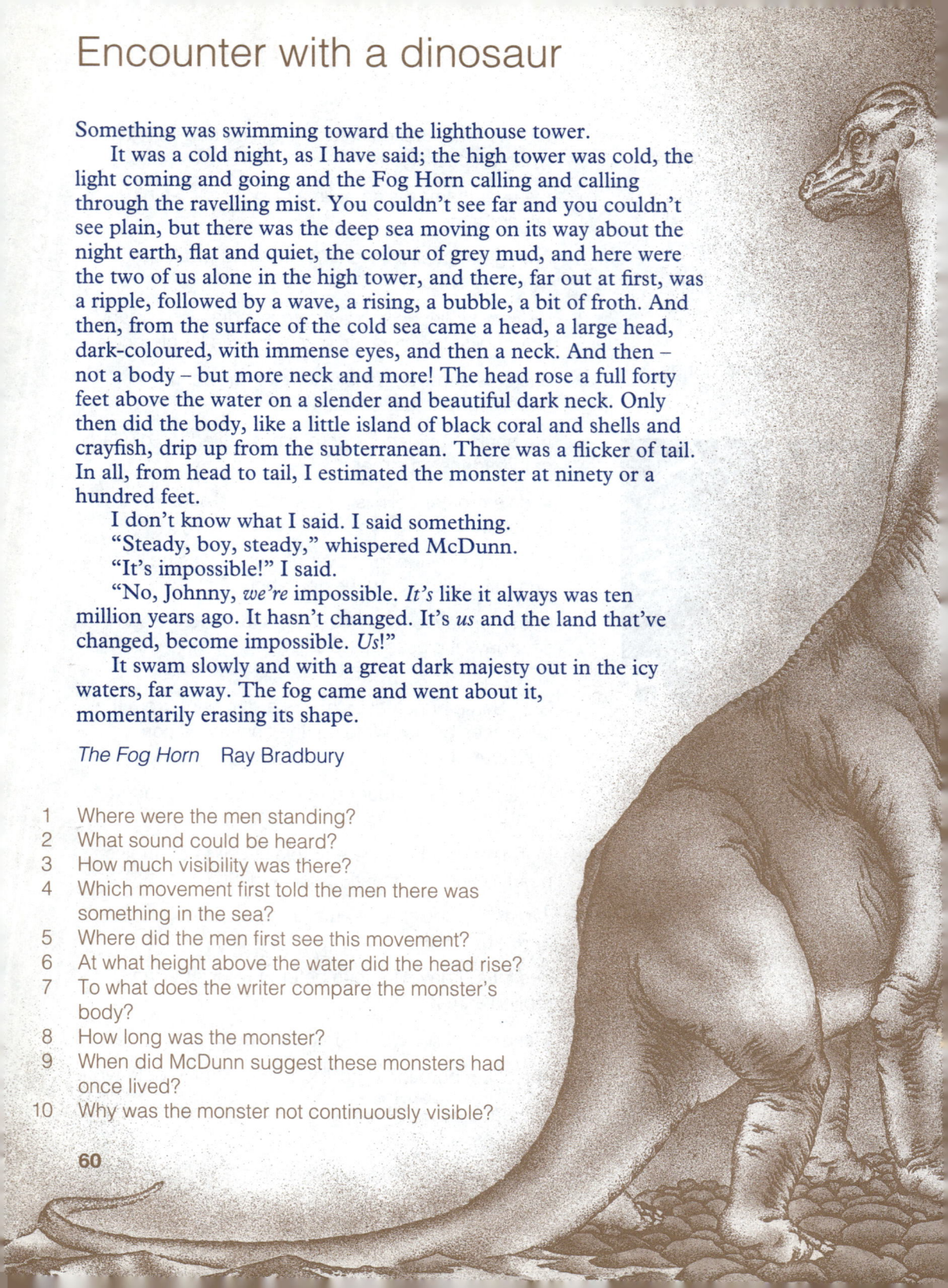

Homophones

herd	a number of animals together
heard	past tense of hear
key	locks a door, etc.
quay	a landing-place for ships
night	time between evening and morning
knight	a titled gentleman
muscle	part of the body
mussel	a shellfish
place	a particular part of space
plaice	a flat-fish
profit	gain; benefit
prophet	one who foretells events
sew	to work with needle and thread
sow	to scatter seed
stile	steps in a fence or wall
style	fashion
vale	a valley
veil	thin material covering face
stationery	writing materials
stationary	standing still

A　Choose the correct word from the pair above to complete each sentence.

1　**vale　veil**
The bride wore a ____ of lace.

2　**stationery　stationary**
The fast sports car collided with a ____ saloon car.

3　**profit　prophet**
The ____ foretold the defeat of the Hebrews.

4　**sow　sew**
In spring farmers plough their fields and ____ the seed.

5　**muscle　mussel**
Having pulled a ____ in his thigh the centre-half had to leave the field.

B　Complete each sentence by using a suitable pair of homophones from your list.

1　The thundering hoofs of the stampeding ____ of buffalo could be ____ from a long way off.

2　The ____ to the sailor's chest was found lying on the ____ .

3　The black ____ rode out one ____ to attack the baron's castle.

4　The athlete vaulted over the ____ in fine ____ .

5　The fishmonger put the huge ____ in a prominent ____ on the marble slab.

Five familiar uses of the comma

1 Commas are used with terms of address.

Examples
"Marva, come here!"
"Yes, sir."
"I think, your majesty, we are lost."

2 Commas are used in lists.

Example
We bought cakes, crisps, sweets and lemonade.

3 Commas are used to separate words and phrases like **oh, well, yes, as a matter of fact,** at the beginning of a sentence.

Example
Well, I did warn you.

4 Commas are used to separate words like **please** at the end of a sentence.

Example
Can you help me, please?

5 Commas are used in the punctuation of direct speech.

Examples
Robert said, "It is getting late."
"It is getting late," said Robert.
"It is getting late," said Robert, "and we should be leaving."

Copy these sentences, adding commas where they are needed.

1 "Your highness your crown is crooked."

2 I have packed sweaters socks and anoraks.

3 "Jake can you hear me?"

4 "Can I help you madam?"

5 "Yes I want to buy a warm vest."

6 I've brushed the stairs I've polished the furniture I've cleaned the windows and now I'm going to have a rest.

7 "Good morning Mrs. Brown."

8 David asked "Are you awake?"

9 "I'm fast asleep" replied Tom quietly.

10 "I know very well" said David "that you're wide awake."

11 "Anna and Matthew it's time for bed."

12 Uncle Fred can speak German French Spanish Italian and Russian.

13 As a matter of fact you are right.

14 "Will you lock the door after you please?"

15 "Hello James."

Rhymes

farms
be
floors
rye
roars
tower
I
arms
see
devour
doors
sails
me
flails
flour

A Write the words, numbered 1 to 15, which fill the spaces in the verses below.

Behold! a giant am ____   1
Aloft here in my ____ .   2
With my granite jaws I ____   3
The maize, and the wheat and the ____ ,   4
And grind them into ____ .   5

I look down over the ____   6
In the fields of grain I ____   7
The harvest that is to ____ ,   8
And I fling to the air my ____   9
For I know it is all for ____ .   10

I hear the sound of ____   11
Far off, from the threshing ____ ,   12
In barns, with their open ____ ,   13
And the wind, the wind in my ____   14
Louder and louder ____ .   15

B Write the word needed to complete each sentence. In each case the missing word rhymes with the word in bold type.

1   He was sorry to have to ____ the invitation.   **fine**

2   She will ____ her hundredth birthday tomorrow. **wait**

3   The architect will ____ the site for the school.   **play**

4   The rabbit was caught in a ____ .   **pair**

5   The ____ against smoking will receive strong support.   **main**

6   Wise parents rarely ____ in the quarrels of their children.   **deer**

7   When you pay a bill you should obtain a ____ . **meet**

8   ____ furniture is very old and often very valuable. **beak**

9   We are going to ____ our parts for the school play. **purse**

10   The tourists stayed at a ____ village in the Alps. **desk**

Prepositions

The dog is **on** the chair.

The dog is **under** the table.

The dog is **in** the car.

The words **in**, **under** and **on** show how the word 'dog' is related to the words **car**, **table** and **chair**.

A word which shows the relationship between a noun (or pronoun) and some other word in a sentence is called a preposition.

above
across
after
against
along
around
at
before
below
beneath
by
for
from
near
of
off
on
outside
over
through
under
up

between

among

in

into

differ

different

A   Insert the prepositions in the list on the left in their correct places in the sentences which follow.

1   Judith is suffering ____ appendicitis.

2   Crowds of people strolled ____ the promenade.

3   Grandpa was seated ____ a blazing fire.

4   Henry leaned ____ the wall of the gymnasium.

5   The dog ran ____ the cat, but could not catch it.

6   Drake was the first Englishman to sail ____ the world.

7   The dog jumped right ____ the hollyhocks.

8   A long queue formed ____ the football ground.

9   Lovely water lilies floated ____ the surface of the pond.

10   A workman fell ____ a ladder and was badly hurt.

Using prepositions correctly

Things are shared between two persons.

Things are shared among more than two.

Shows position in one place.
e.g. The budgie was in its cage.

Shows movement from one place to another.
e.g. The budgie hopped from the table into its cage.

The twins differ **from** each other in some ways.
I beg to differ **with** you on that point.

This book is quite different **from** the one I read last.
(Never use **to** or **than** with different.)

beside	Means by the side of.	
	e.g. Simon sits beside me in school.	
besides	Means in addition to.	
	e.g. Another bicycle was stolen besides John's.	

Note that the same word may be followed by different prepositions.

Examples

a I agree **with** you in everything you say.
I hope you will agree **to** my suggestion.

b The headmaster was angry **with** the children.
He was angry **at** their bad behaviour.

c The soldier died **for** his country.
The soldier died **of** wounds.

d The traveller lives **in** Bournemouth.
He lives **at** 27 Broad Street.

e He would not part **with** a penny.
She hates to part **from** her mother.

B Use a **preposition** to complete each sentence.

1 The children were walking about ____ the classroom.

2 The children went from the playground ____ the classroom.

3 Do you agree ____ this proposal?

4 He will agree ____ everything you say.

5 The prize was divided ____ the two winners.

6 The prize was divided ____ several competitors.

7 Angus now lives ____ Edinburgh.

8 He lives with his aunt ____ 49 Argyll Street.

9 The matron stood ____ the patient's bed.

10 He has a private income ____ his large salary.

C Use these phrases in sentences of your own.

1	walked in	4	walked across
2	walked into	5	walked behind
3	walked on	6	walked under

Tarka fights Deadlock

Between boulders and rocks crusted with shellfish and shaggy with seaweed, past worm-channelled posts that marked the fairway for fishing boats at high water, the pack hunted the otter. Off each post a gull launched itself, cackling angrily as it looked down at the animals. Tarka reached the sea. He walked slowly into the surge of a wavelet, and sank away from the chop of old Harper's jaws, just as Deadlock ran through the pack. Hounds swam beyond the line of waves, while people stood at the sea-lap and watched the huntsman wading to his waist. It was said that the otter was dead-beat, and probably floating stiffly in the shallow water. After a few minutes the huntsman shook his head, and withdrew the horn from his waistcoat. He filled his lungs and stopped his breath and was tightening his lips for the four long notes of the call-off, when a brown head with hard dark eyes was thrust out of the water a yard from Deadlock. Tarka stared into the hound's face and cried "Ic-yang".

The head sank. Swimming under Deadlock, Tarka bit on to the loose skin of the flews and pulled the hound's head under the water. Deadlock tried to twist round and crush the otter's skull in his jaws, but he struggled vainly. Bubbles blew out of his mouth. Soon he was choking. The hounds did not know what was happening. Deadlock's hindlegs kicked the air weakly. The huntsman waded out and pulled him inshore, but Tarka loosened his bite only when he needed new air in his lungs.

Tarka the Otter   Henry Williamson

1   Name three physical features that were part of the shore where the otter was hunted.
2   What made the gulls angry?
3   What were the people standing on the shore doing?
4   What did people think had happened to Tarka?
5   Why did the huntsman shake his head?
6   What did he then prepare to do?
7   What prevented him from performing this action?
8   Why was Deadlock's struggle in vain?
9   What part of Deadlock's body was above the surface of the water?
10   Why did Tarka loosen his bite?
11   Which word in the passage means "navigable channel"?
12   Which word means "the hanging lips of a bloodhound"?

66

Containers

A **caddy** is a container for **tea**.
A **purse** is a container for **money**.

A Write the names of the containers shown in the pictures.

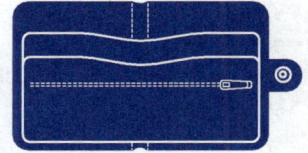

B Write in order the words which have been omitted from these sentences.

1 The carpenter's tools were kept in a large wooden ____ .

2 The china was packed in straw in a large ____ .

3 Penelope poured the contents of two packets of tea into the ____ .

4 There are piles of plates in the kitchen ____ .

5 Sarah hung her best dress in her mother's ____ .

6 The cowboy put his revolver back in its ____ .

7 The archer took an arrow from his ____ .

8 Many walkers carry a ____ on their backs.

9 The ____ in Black Beauty's stable was piled up with hay.

10 Farmer Giles gave the haymakers a ____ of cider.

barrel
caddy
chest
crate
cupboard
dustbin
holster
kitbag
manger
purse
quiver

rucksack
safe
satchel
scabbard
scuttle
sheath
toolbox
vase
wallet
wardrobe

Words with more than one meaning

Some words have more than one meaning.

Example
You should **check** the working of every sum.
The bookmaker wore a **check** suit.

charge	litter
chest	plane
coach	spring
express	stern
ground	temple

A Write the numbers from 1 to 10 in a column, then opposite each write the word which will complete both sentences.

1 The beach was covered with ____ after the vast crowd of holiday-makers had left.
Trixie had a ____ of six lovely puppies.

2 The pirates kept the treasure in a wooden ____ .
A cold on the ____ often makes breathing difficult.

3 The ____ for admission to the circus was £5.
The troops were ordered to ____ the enemy.

4 He could not find words to ____ his thanks.
The ____ train was travelling at 200 kilometres an hour.

5 The ____ was covered with fallen leaves.
The coffee was ____ by machinery.

6 The daffodil is my favourite ____ flower.
The ____ of the clock was broken.

7 A ____ man is very strict and severe.
The ____ of a ship is the rear part.

8 Carpenters ____ wood to make it smooth.
The ____ circled the airport twice before landing.

9 Several Hindus were worshipping in the ____ .
A blow on the ____ rendered the man unconscious.

10 A new teacher had been appointed to ____ the boys at cricket.
The ____ was carrying thirty-five passengers on a school journey.

B Show how these words can have more than one meaning.

1	fly	7	train
2	drop	8	punch
3	plain	9	rule
4	present	10	board
5	bank	11	sink
6	wave	12	pen

Occupations

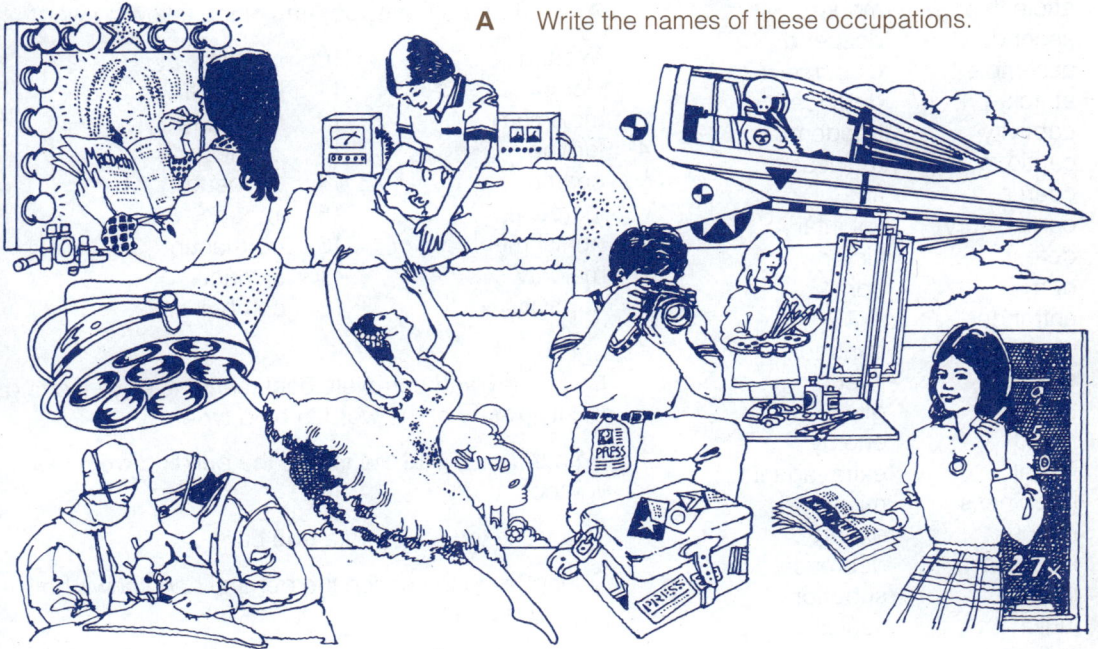

A   Write the names of these occupations.

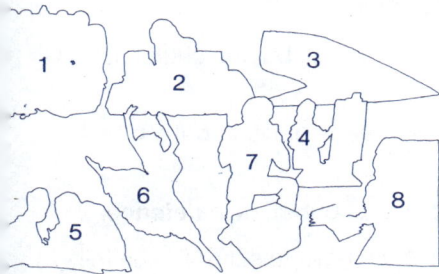

artist	mechanic
actress	messenger
ballerina	optician
beautician	photographer
caddie	physiotherapist
chauffeur	pilot
chiropodist	reporter
conjurer	sculptor
engineer	solicitor
fishmonger	surgeon
interpreter	taxidermist
juggler	teacher
lumberjack	ventriloquist

B   Choose the word in your list which will complete each of these sentences correctly.

1   When the ____ had finished stuffing and mounting the barn owl it looked very lifelike.

2   People who travel in foreign countries often need an ____ to make themselves understood.

3   An exhibition of paintings by a local ____ was held in the town hall.

4   She is a trained ____ specializing in skin care.

5   The ____ was forced to make a crash landing.

6   A number of experienced ____ were consulted about the new bridge.

7   The ____ told the magistrates that her client had been assaulted by the defendant.

8   The ____ collected the tickets at the booking office.

9   He has arthritis and is treated by a ____ each week.

10 The ____ performed the heart transplant successfully.

Antonyms opposites

ancient	modern		
ascend	descend		
assemble	disperse		
attack	defence		
captivity	freedom		
cautious	reckless		
coarse	fine		
compulsory	voluntary		
defeat	victory		
deny	admit		
entrance	exit		
expand	contract		
exterior	interior		
famine	glut		
friend	enemy		
frugal	extravagant		
happiness	misery		
import	export		
increase	decrease		
inferior	superior		
junior	senior		
majority	minority		
maximum	minimum		
permanent	temporary		
present	absent		
punishment	reward		
question	answer		
retreat	advance		
sweet	sour		
transparent	opaque		
vacant	occupied		
vague	precise		
wax	wane		
weak	strong		

A What are the **opposites** of the following words?

1 expand
2 victory
3 maximum
4 famine
5 coarse
6 increase
7 punishment
8 majority
9 captivity

10 inferior
11 entrance
12 transparent
13 cautious
14 descend
15 import
16 permanent
17 exterior
18 compulsory

B Copy and complete each sentence by inserting the **opposite** of the word in bold type.

1 Both the ____ and the **exit** of the building were well lighted.

2 This file is too ____ ; try a **fine** one.

3 During his long service the general had known both ____ and **defeat**.

4 Service with the Armed Forces was ____ for men and **voluntary** for women.

5 The castle is an ____ building, but the church is quite **modern**.

6 The ____ of the house needs painting but the **interior** is perfect.

7 The team is strong in ____ but weak in **defence**.

8 **Cautious** motorists often have to suffer for the folly of the____ .

9 After two years of ____ the prisoners of war thought **freedom** was wonderful.

10 The teacher believed in ____ for the wicked and **reward** for the good.

11 England ____ more goods than it **exports**.

12 **Vague** answers will not do; I need ____ information.

Hyphens

Hyphens join some compound adjectives.

Examples
twenty-eight
happy-go-lucky

Hyphens join some compound nouns.

Examples
horse-box
make-up

Hyphens can indicate that a word continues on the next line.

Example
Sam is always exag-
gerating

It's best NOT to split words if you can avoid it.

Always divide the word at a sensible point between syllables.

The hyphen at the end of a line indicates the word is about to be split. You DON'T need a hyphen on the next line as well.

A   Use hyphens to join the compound adjectives.

1   long lost relation
2   grey green eyes
3   fifty minute tests
4   old fashioned clothes
5   sixty five candles

B   Which compound noun in each trio is correctly punctuated?
Use your dictionary for reference.

1   body building
    body-building
    bodybuilding

2   cup board
    cup-board
    cupboard

3   merry go round
    merry-go-round
    merrygoround

4   public house
    public-house
    publichouse

5   lay by
    lay-by
    layby

C   Which word break is acceptable?

1   ridiculo-   r-   ridicu-
    us   idiculous   lous

2   examina-   examinat-
    tion   ion

D   Use your dictionary to find three examples of compound nouns which have hyphens.

Paragraph topics and sequencing

A paragraph is a series of sentences about the same topic.

Example
If you want to make successful cakes, just remember four simple rules. Firstly, always weigh and measure the ingredients. Secondly, use the right size cake tin. Thirdly, set the oven on the recommended setting. Lastly, wait patiently until the cake is cooked.

Planning a composition means choosing the topics for the paragraphs and arranging them in a sensible order.

A What is the topic of each of these paragraphs?

1 Don't leave everything to the last minute. A project needs careful researching, careful planning and careful presentation. All this takes time and no stage can be left out.

2 My grandfather was a lonely man in many ways, especially after Grandma died. He had few hobbies and found it difficult to make friends. Fortunately, he had his two dogs Gipsy and Rusty, who went everywhere with him. He was 92 when he died. I still miss him.

B Arrange these topics in a sensible order.

1 **The birthday party**
   a Saying goodbye to everyone
   b Blowing out the candles
   c Sending out the invitations
   d Opening the door as everyone arrives
   e Laying the table

2 **A typical Saturday**
   a Watching television until bedtime
   b Unpacking the carrier bags
   c Shopping with my mother
   d Helping to cook supper
   e Tidying my bedroom before breakfast

C **Plan** a composition on a class outing. List your paragraph topics in order.

D Choose three of the topics below and write one paragraph about each.

   a A great football match
   b Your best friend
   c Your favourite meal
   d How to make a sandwich
   e Your favourite place
   f A bad day

Agreement of subject and verb

The **subject** of a sentence must agree with its **verb** in number.

A **singular subject** requires a **singular verb**.

Example
A **cow is** a very useful animal.

A **plural subject** requires a **plural verb**.

Example
Cows are very useful animals.

Now look carefully at this sentence.

A fine **selection** of used cars **was** on view.

The noun **selection**, which is the **subject**, is **singular**, so the singular verb **was** must be used.

Always use a **singular verb** with **each, anybody, nobody, everybody, everyone, no one, either, neither**.

Example
Neither of these knives **is** very sharp.

A   Choose the correct **verb** from the pair above to complete each sentence.

1 **has   have**
   A violet ____ a fragrant smell.

2 **has   have**
   Violets ____ a fragrant smell.

3 **wasn't   weren't**
   The book ____ on the shelf.

4 **wasn't   weren't**
   The books ____ on the shelf.

5 **tries   try**
   The boys ____ hard to make good progress.

6 **tries   try**
   The boy ____ hard to make good progress.

B   Watch for the **subject** in each sentence and use the verb which agrees with it in number.

1 **has   have**
   One of the twins ____ very red hair.

2 **has   have**
   Both of the twins ____ rosy cheeks.

3 **was   were**
   The bunch of keys ____ lost in the street.

4 **was   were**
   The keys ____ lost in the street.

5 **makes   make**
   A box of chocolates ____ a nice present.

6 **makes   make**
   Chocolates ____ a nice present.

7 **is   are**
   Road accidents ____ increasing in number.

8 **is   are**
   The number of road accidents ____ increasing.

Metaphors

Both similes and metaphors describe by making comparisons.

Michael ran down the road **as fast as a hare**. (*Simile*)

Michael **hared** down the road. (*Metaphor*)

A simile explains the comparison and begins with **like**, **as**, **as if** or **as though**.

A metaphor hints at the comparison and leaves you to work it out for yourself.

Examples of metaphors

Anna **flew** downstairs.
What two things are being compared?
Anna and a bird.
How is Anna like a bird?
They both move quickly.

My father **towered** over us.
What two things are being compared?
My father and a tower.
How is my father like a tower?
They are both very tall.

A Each of these sentences contains a metaphor. Explain what is being compared in each, and how the two things are alike.

1 The clouds sailed across the sky.

2 We ducked down out of sight.

3 Jo just skimmed quickly through the book.

4 Matthew wolfed down his lunch in three minutes.

5 My father just exploded when I told him the news.

B Describe a situation where these metaphorical expressions could be used.

1 striking while the iron is hot

2 getting into hot water

3 turning over a new leaf

4 sitting on the fence

5 letting the cat out the bag

Words which save work

One word can sometimes do the work of several.

Example

People who eat more than is good for them are rarely healthy.

Gluttons are rarely healthy.

accidentally
apologized
author
drought
fearlessly
immediately
librarian
occasionally
postponed
recently
revolved
speechless
surrendered
survivors
talkative

A   In each sentence below, replace the words in bold type with a labour-saving word from the list on the left.

1   I met Robert in London **not long ago**.

2   The rebel leader **gave himself up** to the Government forces.

3   Owing to bad weather the school sports had to be **put off to a later date**.

4   Gillian is a bright pupil but rather **fond of talking too much**.

5   After his surprise win Roger was **incapable of speaking**.

6   It is wise to visit the dentist **every now and then**.

7   The **great shortage of rain** has ruined the crops.

8   Of the forty-two passengers in the plane crash, there were only three **who remained alive**.

B

1   The window was broken **by accident**.

2   The hooligans were ordered to leave the cinema **without further delay**.

3   I received a copy of the book of poems from the **man who wrote it**.

4   The policeman tackled the armed robber **without any fear**.

5   Robert asked the **man in charge of the library** if he could recommend the book he had chosen.

6   The chairman of the meeting **expressed his regret** for his late arrival.

7   The blades of the electric fan **turned round and round** at a fantastic speed.

Homophones

bail   **a** money paid to set a person free
       b crosspiece of a wicket

bale a large bundle

berth place to sleep on a ship

birth being born

faint **a** condition like sleep or death
       b weak, not plain

feint a sham blow or attack

gilt thin covering of gold
guilt state of having done wrong

stake a pointed stick
steak a slice of meat or fish

lessen to grow or make less
lesson something learnt or taught

root underground part of a plant

route a way to go; a road

sight power or act of seeing
site position or place

soar to fly upwards or at a great height

sore painful

hoard to save and store up
horde a crowd, e.g. of hooligans

From the list of the left, choose the correct homophone to complete each sentence.

1   We watched the skylark ____ up into the sky.

2   The champion made a ____ with his left then landed with a punishing right hook.

3   Two of the accused men were released on ____ .

4   Our new house is being built on a sunny ____ .

5   On the voyage to America Tony slept on an upper ____ .

6   The prisoner admitted his ____ and was sentenced to three months' imprisonment.

7   No sooner had he scored a goal than he was surrounded by a ____ of hooligans.

8   A strong ____ was driven into the earth to support the young apple tree.

9   The tablets he took did much to ____ the pain in his chest.

10   Before we began our tour, Dad planned the ____ we were to take.

Noises of creatures

A What are the names of the noises made by these creatures?

apes   gibber
bears   growl
bulls   bellow
crows   caw
donkeys   bray
elephants   trumpet
frogs   croak
horses   neigh
hounds   bay
hyenas   laugh; scream
lambs   bleat
mice   squeak
monkeys   chatter
owls   hoot
oxen   low
parrots   screech; talk
rabbits   squeal
snakes   hiss
sparrows   chirp
swallows   twitter
turkeys   gobble

B Write the missing words.

1 horses ____   6 ____ chatter
2 oxen ____   7 ____ laugh
3 bears ____   8 hounds ____
4 ____ gibber   9 ____ chirp
5 ____ bellow   10 ____ gobble

C Write the word needed to complete each sentence, adding **-ing** or **-ed** where required.

1 The pet lamb was ____ for more milk from the bottle.

2 The hounds were ____ with excitement.

3 When the bull ____ the children fled.

4 The continual ____ of the sparrows annoyed Elizabeth.

5 The parrot house at the zoo was filled with the ____ and ____ of these beautiful birds.

6 Judy, the elephant, ____ expectantly as her keeper approached with the food.

7 The old frog ____ contentedly as he hopped about on the edge of the pond.

Johann Gutenberg

Imagine a world without books, newspapers, magazines and all the other printed material we take for granted today. People had none of these things before Johann Gutenberg invented the printing press in the fifteenth century. Although there were a few books available at that time, most people did not have access to them. Each book was handwritten by monks and it took months to produce a single copy. The books they produced were so rare and precious that they were locked away in monastery libraries.

Gutenberg was born in the German town of Mainz where his father was the Master of the Mint. The young boy was fascinated by the way the goldsmiths stamped letters and figures on to coins. Eventually, he became a skilled metalworker himself.

Gutenberg was also interested in the handwritten books in the monastery library. He would spend hours poring over them and watching the monks laboriously copying the scripts. As he watched, an idea came to him. Could a metalwork process be used to produce words on a page? Gutenberg's idea was to cut the letters of the alphabet on individual blocks of metal which could then be moved round to form words. He invented a printing press in which metal letters were fitted into a frame to make up the words on a page.

Gutenberg was a poor man and he needed money to develop his idea. Therefore, he agreed to a proposal put to him by a cunning lawyer named Johann Fust. Fust offered to pay for the printing press, inks and papers Gutenberg needed if he could become Gutenberg's partner.

In 1456, Gutenberg printed 300 copies of the famous *Gutenberg Bible*. This was the start of book publishing and should have made Gutenberg rich and famous. But Fust was greedy, and decided to get rid of his partner. He demanded his money back. Gutenberg could not pay, so Fust seized his equipment and took over the business. Gutenberg did not earn any money from his invention and died penniless twelve years later.

c. 1397	1428	1448	1450	1456	1468
born in Mainz, Germany	moves to Strasbourg and begins to experiment with printing apparatus	returns to Mainz and tries to borrow money for his work	forms partnership with Johann Fust and begins to set up printing press	prints 300 copies of the 1,282 page *Gutenberg Bible*	dies in Mainz

Twenty Inventors   Jacqueline Dineen

1   How were books produced before the printing press was invented?
2   Give two of the reasons why so few people had access to books before the printing press was invented.
3   Which two of Gutenberg's boyhood interests led to his invention?
4   What do you do if you **pore** over a book?
5   What does **laboriously** mean in paragraph three?
6   How was metal used in Gutenberg's printing press?
7   Fust and Gutenberg became partners in 1450. What did each contribute?
8   How many copies of the *Gutenberg Bible* were produced in 1456?
9   How many pages were there in the *Gutenberg Bible*?
0   In what way was Johann Fust greedy?
1   How much money did Gutenberg earn from his invention?
2   Suggest a heading for each paragraph that will accurately sum up what each is about.

Sounds

Object	Sound
anvil	clang
bagpipes	skirl
bell	peal; tinkle
bow	twang
brakes	grinding
bullet	ping
chains	jangle; rattle
coins	chink; jingle
corks	pop
dishes	rattle; clatter
engine	throb
explosion	blast
hinges	creak
rifle	report
silk	rustle
siren	wail
skirts	swish
stream	babble; murmur
thunder	clap; peal
wings	whirr

A Write the missing words; some you learnt in Books 2 and 3.

1 the twang of a ____
2 the call of a ____
3 the tinkle of a ____
4 the jingle of ____
5 the shuffle of ____
6 the rustle of ____
7 the grinding of ____
8 the babble of a ____
9 the lash of a ____
10 the skirl of ____
11 the ____ of skirts
12 the ____ of dishes
13 the ____ of corks
14 the ____ of a bullet
15 the ____ of hoofs
16 the ____ of raindrops
17 the ____ of a rifle
18 the ____ of chains
19 the ____ of an anvil
20 a ____ of thunder

B Write in order the words necessary to complete these sentences.

1 With a noisy ____ of wings thousands of starlings descended on the town.

2 The bridal pair left the church to a merry ____ of bells.

3 The workmen were temporarily deafened by the ____ of the explosion.

4 The frequent ____ of the anvil showed how busy the blacksmith was.

5 When hinges ____ they require oiling.

6 The ____ of the siren announced that a fire had broken out.

7 The Highland regiment marched to the ____ of bagpipes.

8 Derek tossed restlessly in his bunk, disturbed by the ____ of the ship's engines.

Doers of actions

Action	Doer
apply	applicant
auction	auctioneer
burgle	burglar
capture	captor
challenge	challenger
compete	competitor
contribute	contributor
correspond	correspondent
criticize	critic
dictate	dictator
edit	editor
guard	guardian
lie	liar
mutiny	mutineer
operate	operator
oppose	opponent
preside	president
represent	representative
succeed	successor
survive	survivor

Memorize this list, then answer the questions.

A   What word is used for:

1   one who challenges?
2   one who contributes?
3   one who edits?
4   one who presides?
5   one who lies?
6   one who criticizes?
7   one who applies?
8   one who operates?
9   one who competes?
10   one who survives?

B   Complete each sentence by inserting the word for the doer of the action.

1   A ____ broke into the bank last night.   **burgle**

2   The young orphan was accompanied by his ____ .   **guard**

3   In two hours the ____ had sold all the paintings.   **auction**

4   One ____ was shot in the chest.   **mutiny**

5   The prisoner was treated well by his ____ .   **capture**

6   A ____ of the company demonstrated their computer software.   **represent**

7   Some countries do not have a monarch or a president; they have a ____ .   **dictate**

8   In less than a minute the wrestler had thrown his ____ .   **oppose**

9   The retiring caretaker showed his ____ round the school.   **succeed**

10   The film star ordered a photograph to be sent to every ____ .   **correspond**

Three uses of the comma

Look at the examples on the left and see if you can work out **why** the commas have been used. Answers are on the right-hand side of the page.

Examples

Reasons why commas are used

1 The last cottage we saw when we were house-hunting was a little one with thick walls and a squat chimney, and we both fell in love with it.

The comma provides a pause, a chance to get your breath back, in a long sentence.

2 Mrs. Paul, our headmistress, is retiring this term.

The pair of commas encloses supplementary information about Mrs. Paul. It could be omitted or put in brackets.

3 a The boys, who were wearing helmets, were not injured.

The pair of commas shows that all the boys are included.
No boy was injured.
All the boys wore helmets.

   b The boys who were wearing helmets were not injured.

Some boys were injured.
Only those wearing helmets escaped.

A Use one comma in each of these sentences to introduce a pause. (Look back later at the passage to see what the writers did.)

1 Modern agricultural methods include the use of pesticides which effectively control insects classified as pests but which also destroy many that are not. (Page 18)

2 Hounds swam beyond the line of waves while people stood at the sea-lap and watched the huntsman wading to his waist. (Page 66)

3 It swam slowly and with a great dark majesty out in the icy waters far away. (Page 60)

4 The church was very dark and quiet now but not empty because no place that has been used for so long by so many people can ever be empty. (Page 48)

5   Darzee and his wife only cowered down in the nest without answering for from the thick grass at the foot of the bush there came a low hiss – a horrid cold sound that made Rikki-tikki jump back two clear feet. (Page 24)

B   Read this pair of sentences and answer the question that follows.

The girls who washed up were thanked by their teacher.
The girls, who washed up, were thanked by their teacher.

Which sentence means that <u>all</u> the girls were thanked because <u>all</u> the girls washed up?

C   Copy these sentences, putting in the pair of commas needed in each to enclose supplementary information.

1   My dog a bulldog terrifies everyone.

2   Prince Charles the Queen's eldest son is heir to the throne.

3   The prize a trip to Alton Towers was won by the headmaster.

4   I had my favourite meal fish fingers and chips since it was my birthday.

5   Her best friend Zena Partridge is leaving.

A fight in a signal-tower

Up over the edge of the spur, three wild horsemen appeared heading for the gateway.

As they dropped from their ponies in the courtyard below, Marcus and Esca drew back from the parapet. "Only three, so far," Marcus whispered. "Don't use your knife unless you have to. They may be of more use to us living than dead."

Esca nodded, and returned his hunting-knife to his belt. Life and the urgency of doing had taken hold of them again. Flattened against the wall on either side of the stairhead they waited, listening to their pursuers questing through storehouse and guardroom. "Fools!" Marcus breathed, as a shout told them that the stairway had been spotted; and then came a rush of feet that checked at the floor below and then came on, storming upward.

Marcus was a good boxer, and much practice with the cestus last winter had made Esca something of a boxer also; together, weary though they were, they made a dangerous team. The first two tribesmen to come ducking out through the low doorway went down without a sound, like poled oxen; the third, not so completely caught unawares, put up more of a fight. Esca flung himself upon him, and they crashed down several steps together, in a flailing mass of arms and legs. There was a short, desperate struggle before Esca came uppermost, and staggering clear, heaved an unconscious man over the doorsill.

The Eagle of the Ninth   Rosemary Sutcliff

1 Where were Marcus and Esca when the horsemen appeared?
2 Where did the horsemen dismount?
3 Which words suggest there might have been more horsemen to come?
4 Why did Marcus advise Esca not to use his knife?
5 Where did Esca keep his knife?
6 Where were their pursuers searching for them?
7 Why did Marcus describe their pursuers as fools?
8 What kind of training had made Esca into a boxer?
9 Why did the third tribesman put up more of a fight than the other two?
10 In what state was the third tribesman after the fight?

Double negatives

Words containing **not** or **no** are called **negatives**.

Examples
no   not   nobody   nothing
nowhere   none   never *(not ever)*

Two negatives should never be used together in the same sentence.

Wrong
He did **not** tell me **nothing** about it. *(two negatives)*

Right
He did **not** tell me anything about it. *(one negative)*

He told me **nothing** about it. *(one negative)*

Choose the correct word from the pair above to complete each sentence.

1 **nothing   anything**
John did not tell his father ____ about the accident.
John told his father ____ about the accident.

2 **nowhere   anywhere**
We couldn't find the book ____ .
The book was ____ to be found.

3 **nothing   anything**
The gardener didn't pay Tom ____ for his help.
The gardener paid Tom ____ for his help.

4 **never   ever**
Don't you ____ get tired of knitting?
Do you ____ get tired of knitting?

5 **nothing   anything**
We could not see ____ from where we stood.
We could see ____ from where we stood.

6 **no   any**
There isn't ____ cake left.
There is ____ cake left.

7 **nobody   anybody**
We didn't meet ____ on the way home.
We met ____ on the way home.

8 **no   any**
Haven't you ____ sympathy for him?
Have you ____ sympathy for him?

9 **none   any**
I asked Bill for a sweet but he didn't have ____ .
I asked Bill for a sweet but he had ____ .

10 **no one   anyone**
We can't find ____ to dig our garden.
We can find ____ to dig our garden.

11 **nothing   anything**
There isn't ____ wrong with this car.
There is ____ wrong with this car.

12 **no   any**
I looked everywhere but couldn't find ____ bluebells.
I looked everywhere but could find ____ bluebells.

85

More metaphors

Read this sentence and try to work out how the comparison between Miss James's voice and ice helps us to visualize the scene more clearly:

Miss James spoke with an **icy** voice.

The comparison makes the scene more vivid because we all know how cold ice makes us feel. We therefore know the effect of Miss James's voice on those listening.

Metaphors make descriptions more vivid because they compare something we know well with something we can then imagine and understand.

A   All the examples of metaphors in the exercise below have been taken from passages in this book. You will have read most of them already. Now take the time to think carefully about how the metaphors help you to understand the descriptions better.

The metaphor in each sentence is in bold type. Explain how the metaphors help to make the descriptions more vivid.

1   The light **ebbed** from the church. *(Page 48)*

2   The fog came and went about it, momentarily **erasing** its shape. *(Page 60)*

3   "Thanks awfully, but I ought to **stick** by Toad till this trip is ended." *(Page 12)*

4   The strange fragrance was stronger now, coming over the top of the rise in a **wave** of scent that struck him powerfully. *(Page 6)*

5   The first two tribesmen to come **ducking** out through the low doorway went down without a sound. *(Page 84)*

B   Look at each sentence below. From the three words in bold type above each sentence, choose the most appropriate metaphor. Then explain in your own words why the metaphor you have chosen is a good one.

1   **flood   wave   surge**
Tim felt a ____ of embarrassment when he saw all his friends were laughing at him.

2   **enveloped   shrouded   parcelled**
The graveyard was ____ in mist.

3   **wolfed   pigged   gobbled**
My dog Digger ____ all the sausages.

4   **flew   sang   soared**
As I got near home my heart ____ with excitement.

Rhymes

in
kin
admire
attire
thin
pin
bigger
figure
head
red
skin
chin

A   Write the words, numbered from 1 to 12, which fill the spaces in this extract from a poem.

"Come in," the Mayor cried, looking _____ : 1
And in did come the strangest _____ ! 2
His queer long coat from heel to _____ , 3
Was half of yellow and half of _____ , 4
And he himself was tall and _____ , 5
With sharp blue eyes, each like a _____ , 6
And light loose hair, yet swarthy _____ , 7
No tuft on cheek, nor beard on _____ , 8
But lips where smiles went out and _____ ; 9
There was no guessing his kith and _____ 10
And nobody could enough _____ 11
The tall man and his quaint _____ . 12

B   Each of these lines contains three rhyming words from which some of the letters are missing. Complete each word.

Example   1   work
                     jerk
                     shirk

1 work	2 home	3 grows
j _ _ _	f _ _ _	ch _ _ _
sh _ _ _	c _ _ _	fr _ _ _

4 course	5 become	6 stole
f _ _ _ _	cr _ _ _	sh _ _ _
h _ _ _ _ _	gl _ _	scr _ _ _

7 nurse	8 cheer	9 bought
v _ _ _ _	sm _ _ _	c _ _ _ _ _
w _ _._ _	sph _ _ _	t _ _ _

C   Write as eight lines of poetry:

I have a garden of my own, shining with flowers of every hue; I loved it dearly while alone, but I shall love it more with you: and there the golden bees shall come in summer-time at break of morn, and wake us with their busy hum, around the Silea's fragrant thorn.

Direct speech revision

Revise the punctuation of direct speech by looking at the examples below before you do the exercises.

Speech first
"I feel very tired," said Anne.
"Don't do that!" shouted Mark.
"Are you mad?" I asked.

Speech last
Anne said, "I feel very tired."
Mark shouted, "Don't do that!"
I asked, "Are you mad?"

An interrupted sentence of speech
"Nobody will ever know," he whispered, "what happened to the man."

A speech of more than one sentence
"I feel very tired. I am going to bed," said Anne.
Anne said, "I feel very tired. I am going to bed."
"I feel very tired," said Anne. "I am going to bed."

Dialogue
(Remember to start a new line for each new speaker.)
"Hi, Charles," said Stephen.
"Hi," said Charles.
"What are you doing?" asked Stephen.
"Nothing, really," replied Charles.

A   Each sentence contains one punctuation error. Write the sentences correctly.

1   "How are you?" Asked Anne.

2   "I feel a bit sick" I said.

3   "Would you like to lie down," she said kindly.

4   The shopkeeper smiled and murmured "What can I do for you, madam?"

5   "Just as we turned off the main road," said Elaine "a huge coach came roaring towards us!"

B   Supply any missing punctuation marks and write out this conversation between Silver and Hazel, spacing it correctly. When you have finished, look at Page 6 to see how the author, Richard Adams, presented it.

Not asleep, Silver he said. It's too dangerous, Hazel replied Silver. I'd like to sleep as much as anyone but if we all sleep and something comes, who's going to spot it? I know. I've found a place where we can sleep safely for as long as we like. A burrow? No, not a burrow. A great field of scented plants that will cover us, sight and smell, until we're rested. Come out here and smell it, if you like.

Idioms

Learn this list of idioms and their meanings, then work the test which follows.

Idiom	Meaning
to send to Coventry	to ignore a person
to play second fiddle	to take a back place while someone else leads
to take French leave	to go off without permission
to be at loggerheads	to be quarrelling
to make a mountain out of a molehill	to make trifling difficulties appear great ones
to feather one's nest	to increase one's possessions
to pay through the nose	to pay too high a price
to smell a rat	to be suspicious
to give a person the cold shoulder	to make him or her feel unwelcome
to blow one's own trumpet	to boast about oneself

Rewrite these sentences substituting for the words in bold type one of the **idioms** in the list.

1 Mr. Robinson paid **far too high a price** for his car.

2 It is wrong to think only of **adding to one's possessions**.

3 Some people prefer **to take a back place and let someone else take the lead**.

4 Very soon the police began **to be suspicious**.

5 Alan is too fond of **boasting about himself**.

6 The two neighbours are forever **quarrelling**.

7 Faint-hearted people often like making **difficulties appear much greater than they really are**.

8 The bully's mates **ignored him and refused to talk to him**.

9 The soldier took **the week-end off without the permission of his commanding officer**.

10 The old couple decided to give the tramp **the impression that he was most unwelcome**.

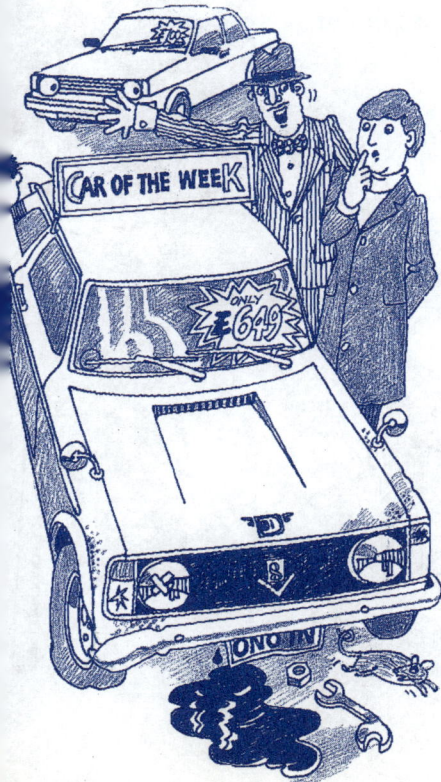

Long John Silver

Long John Silver, our ship's cook – Barbecue, as the men called him – carried his crutch by a lanyard round his neck, to have both hands as free as possible. It was something to see him wedge the foot of his crutch against a bulkhead, and, propped against it, yielding to every movement of the ship, get on with his cooking like someone safe ashore. Still more strange was it to see him in the heaviest of weather cross the deck. He had a line or two rigged up to help him across the widest spaces, and he would hand himself from one place to another, as quickly as another man could walk.

"He's no common man, Barbecue," said the coxswain to me. "He had good schooling in his young days, and can speak like a book when so minded, and he's brave – a lion's nothing alongside of Long John! I've seen him grapple four men, and knock their heads together – and him unarmed."

All the crew respected and even obeyed him. He had a way of doing everybody some particular service. To me he was unweariedly kind; and always glad to see me in the galley.

"Hawkins," he would say, "come and have a yarn with John. Nobody more welcome than yourself, my son. Here's Cap'n Flint – I calls my parrot Cap'n Flint after the famous buccaneer – here's Cap'n Flint predicting success to our voyage. Wasn't you, cap'n?"

And the parrot would say, with great rapidity, "Pieces of eight! pieces of eight! pieces of eight!" till you wondered that it was not out of breath, or till John threw his handkerchief over the cage.

Treasure Island   Robert Louis Stevenson

1   What nickname did the crew give Long John Silver?
2   How did John carry his crutch?
3   Why did he carry it in this way?
4   How did he use his crutch when cooking?
5   What helped John to cross the widest spaces of the deck in the heaviest weather?
6   What example of John's bravery did the coxswain give?
7   Why did the crew respect John?
8   What was the name of John's parrot?
9   What is another word for "buccaneer"?
10   How did John stop the parrot talking?

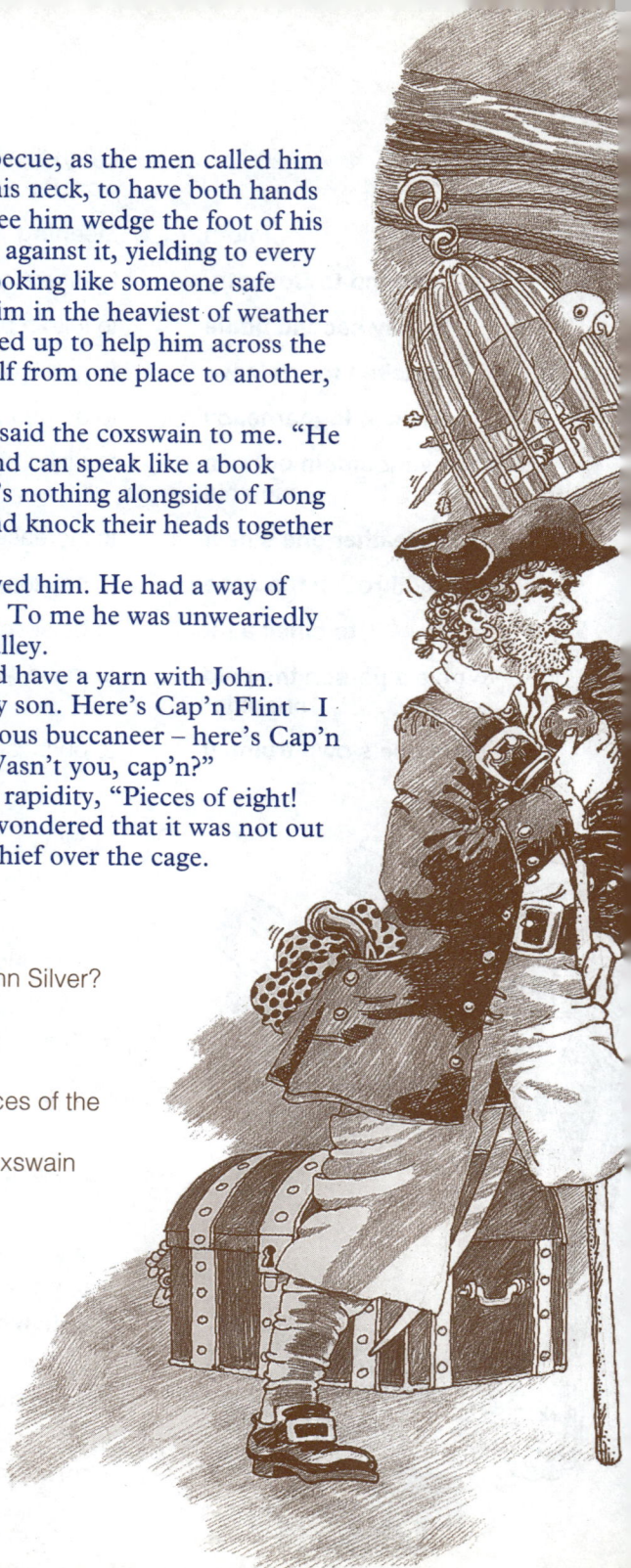

Answers

Page 1   Nouns

A

milkfloat
tyres
wheels
steering-wheel
windscreen
windscreen-wiper
lights
nameboard
lettering
driving-seat
milk
milk-bottles

crates
milkman
cap
shirt
tie
trousers
jacket
shoes
cat
house
roof

chimneys
windows
door
gate
woman
fence
trees
shrubs
path
clouds
birds

B

1 car; ice; tree
2 diamonds; rubies; emeralds; stones
3 players; team
4 dog; man; friend
5 city; country; capital
6 heart; blood; body
7 rust; oxygen; air
8 referee; player; field

C

1 restaurant
2 helicopter
3 palette
4 triangle
5 dollar

Page 2   Verbs

A

1 breathe
2 hibernate
3 wake; search
4 digging; raked
5 produces; exports
6 struck; sank

B

apologize	to express regret	fortify	to make strong
bewilder	to confuse completely	glare	to stare in anger
comprehend	to understand	hibernate	to spend the winter asleep
confess	to own up to a sin	inhale	to breathe in
confide	to tell as a secret	loathe	to regard with disgust
demolish	to pull or tear down	meditate	to think quietly
devour	to eat like an animal	pester	to annoy; to irritate
discuss	to talk over	relax	to become less stiff or firm
expose	to uncover; to lay open	strive	to work hard or try hard
extinguish	to put out; to wipe out	unite	to join together

Page 3   Adjectives

A

1 tame; affectionate
2 sound; ripe; dry; clean
3 Canadian; vast; huge
4 Tame; sociable; quarrelsome
5 short; webbed; thick
6 rough; interlocking

B

arrogant	boastfully proud
boisterous	very noisy and disorderly
contemptuous	very scornful
distinguished	well-known; famous
elaborate	worked out with great care
frantic	wild with rage or pain
gorgeous	richly coloured; splendid
hospitable	giving a warm welcome
intelligent	quick at learning
laborious	requiring much work

memorable	not to be forgotten
obstinate	stubborn
pompous	self-important
ponderous	heavy and clumsy
prosperous	successful; thriving
radiant	bright; shining
repulsive	causing strong dislike
stagnant	not running or flowing
stationary	not moving
tumultuous	rough; violent

Page 4   Adverbs

A

1 carefully *how*
2 frequently *when*
3 away *where*
4 aimlessly *how*
5 shortly *when*
6 noisily *how*

B

1 violently
2 patiently
3 merrily
4 bitterly
5 awkwardly
6 courageously
7 frugally
8 hungrily
9 contentedly
10 politely
11 mournfully
12 uproariously
13 gracefully
14 soundly
15 intimately

Page 5   Nouns – number

A

1 pianos
2 sheaves
3 chimneys
4 heroes
5 mice
6 diaries
7 geese
8 photos
9 thieves
10 chiefs
11 deer
12 discos
13 factories
14 sons-in-law
15 men

B

1 factories
2 turkeys
3 chiefs
4 potatoes
5 thieves
6 wolves
7 pianos
8 deer
9 oxen
10 mice

C

1 The thieves removed the turkeys from the shelves.
2 The chiefs put away their knives.
3 The heroes had their photos taken.
4 The children looked at the little white mice.
5 The foxes looked longingly at the geese.

Pages 6 and 7   Attacked by a crow

1   The scent of the beanfield was just as powerful and unforgettable as the scent of orange-blossom.
2   Broad bean flowers are black and white.
3   One reason why it would be safe to sleep in the beanfield is that the rabbits would be completely hidden from predators.
    The second reason is that no predator would smell them there because the scent of the broad bean flowers is so strong.
4   Bigwig and Silver had been keeping watch.
5   Silver was closest to the beanfield.
6   The crow had chosen Pipkin and Fiver for attack because they were so small and tired and had lagged behind the others.
7   The crow aimed at Fiver with its great bill.
8   Pipkin buried his head in a clump of rank grass.
9   Hazel ran to Pipkin's aid.
10 He succeeded in distracting the crow's attention.
11 He compares it to the sound of a snail-shell when a thrush beats it on a stone.
12 Silver and the crow stood face to face.
13 Bigwig ran straight into the crow from behind and knocked it sideways.

Pages 8 and 9   Verbs – past tense and past participles

A

1	fought	3	slew	5	hurt	7	mistook
2	fled	4	laid	6	wove	8	drowned

B

1	gone	3	hurt	5	woven	7	shown
2	thought	4	chosen	6	hanged	8	frozen

C

1	bore	3	blown	5	drove	7	lay
2	broken	4	begun	6	beaten	8	wrung

Page 10   Sentences, clauses and phrases

A

1	sentence	3	clause	5	sentence	7	phrase
2	phrase	4	sentence	6	clause	8	sentence

B
Own answers.

Page 11   Nouns – gender

A

1	madam	4	mayoress	7	marchioness	9	niece
2	mare	5	peahen	8	cow	10	heiress
3	lady	6	empress				

B

1	drake	4	wizard	7	nephew	9	buck
2	boar	5	stag	8	ram	10	emperor
3	widower	6	colt				

C

1	Empress; daughters	4	aunt; her; niece
2	peahen	5	marchioness
3	woman	6	Madam

D

1	cows	4	Lady
2	duck	5	ewe
3	bull	6	hind

Pages 12 and 13   Toad and company

1   Toad made Rat and Mole catch the old grey horse.
2   The job was difficult because the horse didn't want to be caught.
3   Toad hung nose-bags, nets of onions, bundles of hay and baskets from the bottom of the cart.
4   The animals were sitting on the shaft.
5   They stopped for the night on a common miles from anywhere.
6   They turned the horse loose to graze.
7   They ate their supper sitting on the grass.
8   Boasted means **talked big**.
9   We know Rat is feeling homesick because he admits sadly that he is thinking all the time about the river where he lives.
10   He won't leave Toad because he knows Toad can't look after himself without help.
11   Mole sets off to buy breakfast.
12   They would probably be thinking indignantly that it might be a pleasant easy life as far as Toad was concerned but that they had done all the work.
13   Possibly: boastful, selfish, inefficient, lazy, insensitive, changeable, ungrateful, enthusiastic.

Page 14   Adjectives – formation

	A		**B**		**C**		**D**
1	fluffy	1	stony	1	furry	1	icy
2	squeaky	2	wavy	2	tinny	2	wiry
3	starchy	3	greasy	3	knotty	3	spotty
4	wealthy	4	breezy	4	boggy	4	hazy
5	frosty	5	tasty	5	witty	5	sandy
		6	pebbly	6	skinny	6	foggy

Page 15 Nouns – formation

A

1	imagination	6	astonishment
2	advice	7	decision
3	explosion	8	pronunciation
4	destruction	9	accusation
5	favouritism	10	complaint

B

1	choice	6	pursuit
2	abolition	7	inquiry
3	decision	8	completion
4	explanation	9	deceit
5	satisfaction	10	improvement

Page 16 Other words for said and asked

A

1 … remarked the old boatman
2 … whispered her mother
3 … urged his teacher
4 … shouted the skipper
5 … stammered the frightened boy
6 … admitted Kai Man
7 … boasted Alan
8 … announced the headmaster

B

1 … ordered the surgeon
2 … inquired the stranger
3 … replied the policeman
4 … pleaded Elizabeth
5 … protested the customer
6 … prophesied Aunt Jane
7 … complained the farmer
8 … grumbled the shop assistant

Page 17 Collective nouns

A

1	choir	6	swarm; plague
2	staff	7	crowd
3	brood	8	gang
4	peal	9	pride
5	company	10	flight

B

1	angels	6	minstrels
2	trees	7	arrows
3	stars	8	magistrates
4	pilgrims	9	worshippers
5	directors	10	eggs

C

1	band	4	clump
2	plague; swarm	5	company
3	brood	6	gang

7	board	10	flight
8	crowd	11	congregation
9	host	12	set

Page 18   Wildlife in danger

1   Some species of wild animal may become extinct because streams and rivers have become polluted and because pesticides intended for killing insects that are pests also destroy many that are not. (An increase in building has disturbed and destroyed much of the countryside that provides homes for wild animals. Many species of wild animal are hunted and killed by man for pleasure or for profit.)
2   Factories contribute to the problem if they discharge waste into streams and rivers and so pollute the water.
3   A **pesticide** is a substance designed to kill harmful insects.
4   The increase in population has resulted in an increase in building, and many acres of countryside have been lost to wildlife.
5   It is under threat because it is hunted by sportsmen.
6   Borneo and Sumatra have smuggling problems.
7   The chinchilla is hunted for its fur.
8   Whales are hunted for the oil and food they yield.
9   Sewage pollution has been greatly reduced.
10   A ban on trading in some furs has been agreed. (Organisations like Friends of the Earth have been formed and do valuable work.)
11   Possible answers:
Para. 1 A worldwide problem
Para. 2 The hazards to wildlife
Para. 3 What is being done to help

Page 19   Fun with words

A

					B	
1	**a** harp	6	**a** port		1	S C A M P
	b harpoon		**b** portion		2	C O M E S
2	**a** monk	7	**a** halt		3	P A N I C
	b monkey		**b** halter		4	S N I P E
3	**a** kid	8	**a** host		5	S P A C E
	b kidnap		**b** hostile		6	5 4 7 1 8
4	**a** hat	9	**a** boy		7	2 7 1 6 8
	b hatchet		**b** boycott		8	8 7 3 5 1
5	**a** cent	10	**a** mass		9	7 3 4 6 2
	b centre		**b** massacre		10	8 5 2 6 1

Page 20   Using the right adjective

A

a

1	frantic	6	injurious
2	antique	7	threadbare
3	affectionate	8	meagre
4	formidable	9	precipitous
5	palatable	10	relentless

b

1	struggles	6	drugs
2	furniture	7	clothes
3	daughter	8	allowance
4	task	9	slope
5	meal	10	grip

B

1	vivid	4	shrewd	7	abundant	9	secluded
2	luscious	5	sumptuous	8	candid	10	righteous
3	prosperous	6	riotous				

Page 21   Pronouns

A

1	she; her	5	He; them
2	he; it	6	they
3	We	7	his
4	us		

B

1	yourselves	4	myself
2	yourself	5	herself
3	itself	6	ourselves

Page 22   Homophones

A

1	cereal	4	heir
2	currant	5	brake
3	foul		

B

1	cheque; check	4	course; coarse
2	boy; buoy	5	beach, beech
3	aloud; allowed		

Page 23   Abbreviations

A

1 Member of Parliament
2 Department
3 National Society for the Prevention of Cruelty to Children
4 care of
5 Her Royal Highness
6 Royal Society for the Prevention of Cruelty to Animals
7 as soon as possible
8 Justice of the Peace

B

1 Telephone
2 On Her Majesty's Service
3 Royal Navy (Naval)
4 Automobile Association
5 United Nations
6 Managing Director

C

1 facsimile
2 General Practitioner
3 rest in peace (Latin *requiescat in pace*)
4 anonymous
5 headquarters

Page 24   Rikki-tikki and Darzee

1 He licked his lips because he had found a splendid hunting-ground.
2 His tail grew more bushy and bristly at the thought of it.
3 Rikki-tikki heard very sorrowful voices in a thornbush.
4 The name is appropriate because tailors stitch clothes, and these birds stitch leaves together to make nests.
5 They were crying because one of their babies had fallen out of the nest and Nag had eaten him.
6 The low hiss came from the thick grass at the foot of the bush.
7 They cowered down in the nest.
8 It made him jump back two clear feet.
9 Nag was five feet long from tongue to tail.
10 The cobra ate a tailor-bird chick the day before.
   The cobra is five feet long.
   It can move very slowly.
   It is black.
   It makes a hissing sound.
   It can make part of its head larger when angry.

Page 25   Letter writing

Own answers.

Page 26   Occupations

A

| 1 | waitress | 3 | cricketer | 5 | librarian | 7 | butcher |
| 2 | steeplejack | 4 | announcer | 6 | nurse | 8 | plumber |

B

1	librarian	4	chemist	7	butcher	9	coastguard
2	tobacconist	5	jeweller	8	steeplejack	10	nurse
3	waitress	6	florist				

Page 27 Group names

A

1	vehicles	3	tools	5	crockery	6	footwear
2	vegetables	4	cutlery				

B

1 venison; names of meats
2 synagogue; places of worship
3 alligator; names of reptiles
4 villa; kinds of dwellings
5 silver; names of metals
6 baker; kinds of traders

C

Clothes	Vessels	Furniture	Footwear
shirt	liner	cupboard	clogs
scarf	trawler	table	sandals
tights	submarine	armchair	shoes
vest	schooner	sideboard	boots
trousers	yacht	wardrobe	slippers
jeans	cruiser	cabinet	wellingtons

Pages 28 and 29 Comparing adjectives

A

	Positive degree	Comparative degree	Superlative degree
1	lovely	lovelier	loveliest
2	large	larger	largest
3	hot	hotter	hottest
4	noisy	noisier	noisiest
5	slim	slimmer	slimmest
6	wise	wiser	wisest
7	wet	wetter	wettest
8	wealthy	wealthier	wealthiest
9	fine	finer	finest
10	greedy	greedier	greediest

B

1 more capable
2 most intelligent
3 more generous
4 most expensive
5 more dangerous
6 most wonderful
7 most important
8 more interesting

C

1	worst	3	better	5	best	7	smallest
2	worse	4	worse	6	most	8	less

Pages 30 and 31 William's workshop

1 William is going home at the end of school.
2 He looks fearfully behind him because he suspects that Danny and Laura are following him.
3 His workshop is a garden shed.
4 Danny mentions: computers that talk and do your homework; robot dogs that bark and fetch your slippers; a space rocket.
5 Own answer that must be supported by textual evidence.
6 Own answer that must be supported by textual evidence.
7 Own answer that must be supported by textual evidence.
8 Own answer that must be supported by textual evidence.
9 sarcastically – sneeringly
   incredible – impossible to believe
   robot – machine that can work like a real dog
10 Laura likes calling names and chiming in after Danny. She says spiteful things and quotes what William's teacher has said about him. She doesn't seem as intelligent as Danny; she makes shorter less imaginative remarks. She's more of a follower than a leader, but nevertheless she's unkind and means to hurt William.
11 Own answer.

Page 32 Writing a playscript

A
Answer along these lines:
RIKKI-TIKKI: What is the matter?
   DARZEE: (Sadly) We are very miserable. One of our babies fell out of the nest yesterday, and Nag ate him.
RIKKI-TIKKI: H'm! That is very sad – but I am a stranger here. Who is Nag?

B
Own answer.

C
Own answer.

D
Answer along these lines:
   "More excuses!" Laura sneered. "He's just trying to wriggle out of it!"
   Then Danny asked William, "So what is this big invention, then? Is it a space rocket or something? A rocket that'll fly you to Mars?"
   "Don't be silly," William said quietly. "I couldn't make one of those in my workshop."
   Danny wasn't listening to William's reply. He went on, "Because if it's a space rocket, you could fly it to school, William. Fly it to school and land on the football field!"
   Then Laura chimed in once again. "Anyway, your workshop's not even a proper workshop. It's a crumbly old garden shed!"

Page 33   People

A

1	hypocrite	4	lunatic
2	traitor	5	exile
3	tyrant		

B

1	prophet	4	vandal
2	pedestrian	5	mimic
3	genius		

Page 34   Proper adjectives

A

1	Spanish	4	Chinese	7	Maltese	9	Alpine
2	Greek	5	Dutch	8	Norwegian	10	Swedish
3	Venetian	6	Israeli				

B

1	Greek	4	Swiss	7	Icelandic	9	Alpine
2	Mexican	5	Turkish	8	Venetian	10	Finnish
3	Belgian	6	Portuguese				

Page 35   Nouns – possession

A

1 Ann's dress
2 the knight's sword
3 the tailor's thimble
4 the butcher's shop
5 the cricketer's pads
6 the lion's jaws
7 the winner's reward
8 the boxer's gloves
9 the comedian's jokes

B

1 the clowns' trousers
2 the elephants' tusks
3 the sailors' uniforms
4 the dogs' bones
5 the girls' toys
6 the monkeys' tails
7 the insects' wings
8 the birds' nests
9 the ladies' cloakroom

C

1 women's handbags
2 the oxen's yokes
3 the mice's tails
4 the policemen's helmets
5 children's toys
6 men's shoes
7 the airmen's camp
8 the frogmen's feet
9 the geese's honks

Page 36   Sea-lions

1 A sea-lion is bigger.
2 A fully grown sea-lion is from twelve to twenty feet long.
3 A sea-lion's skin is about an inch in thickness.
4 At least a foot of fat lies between the skin and its flesh or bones.
5 The tail and fins serve the sea-lion for feet.
6 The sea-lion is at sea all the summer.
7 It is on shore all the winter.
8 Young sea-lions are born in the winter.
9 The male has a large trunk or snout, hanging down five or six inches, which the female has not.
10 The males fight chiefly about their females.

Page 37   Contractions

A
1 they'd
2 we'd
3 you'd
4 he'd
5 she'd
6 I'd

B
1 I'm
2 you've
3 she's
4 won't
5 he'd
6 don't
7 they're
8 shan't
9 we've
10 it's
11 haven't
12 she'll
13 I'd
14 we're
15 aren't
16 you're
17 we'd
18 they've
19 can't
20 they'll

C
1 cannot; I am
2 we are
3 you are
4 We have; We will

Page 38   Antonyms – opposites

A
1 sorrow
2 spendthrift
3 expensive
4 deny
5 forbid
6 knowledge
7 innocent
8 retreat
9 solid
10 departure
11 timid
12 humble
13 true
14 scarce
15 success
16 wealth
17 loiter
18 reveal

B
1 expensive
2 absent
3 false
4 shallow
5 loiters
6 guilty

C
1 guilty
  innocent
2 plentiful
  scarce
3 forbid
  permit
4 timid
  bold
5 poverty
  wealth
6 unknown
  famous
7 enthusiastic
  apathetic
8 stop
  start
9 sell
  purchase

Page 39   Direct and indirect speech

A

1   Matthew asked if he could have a bicycle for his birthday.
2   Mr. Dean said that he had a bad headache and that he thought he would lie down.
3   Mr. Caldwell remarked that the days were certainly getting longer.
4   David asked Roger if he knew how to play darts.
5   Mrs. Smith told her son that he looked as if he could do with a good holiday.
6   Peter's mother ordered him to tuck his shirt in.
7   The old lady invited Mrs. Dale to go inside and have tea with them.

B

1   "Your shoes will be ready by Saturday," the shoe repairer told Robert.
2   "Have you loitered on the way home from school, Simon?" asked his mother.
3   "Have you ever spent a holiday in France, Bernard?" asked his teacher.
4   "I once went on a day trip to Dieppe," replied Bernard.
5   "Your work is improving," the headmaster told the boys.
6   "I have come top in English," Judith told her father.
7   "If you stop biting your nails for three months, I'll give you ten pounds," promised her father.
8   "I am feeling tired," said my mother.
9   "I should love to come," I said.
10 "You'd better stay home from school," the doctor advised me.

Page 40   Opposites – using a prefix

A

1   insane
2   unaware
3   inhuman
4   unusual
5   disobedient
6   disapprove
7   inequality
8   dissimilar
9   uncertain
10 imperfect
11 ingratitude
12 disregard
13 discontinue
14 inconsiderate
15 disorderly

B

1   improbable
2   immovable
3   ungrateful
4   illegal
5   irresponsible
6   unnecessary
7   unfortunate
8   discourteous

C

Own answers, using the phrases below.

1   an unpopular man
2   irregular attendance
3   an inefficient worker
4   an unimportant town
5   unfavourable weather
6   an improper remark

Page 41 Diminutives

A

1 elver
2 gosling
3 calf
4 lamb
5 leveret
6 streamlet
7 owlet
8 foal
9 puppy
10 codling
11 tadpole
12 fawn
13 calf
14 rivulet
15 filly
16 cub
17 eaglet
18 cygnet

B

1 elvers
2 filly (foal)
3 hare
4 horse (mare)
5 sheep
6 calf
7 cygnets
8 kittens

Page 42 The Royal Mint

1 Bristol, Canterbury, London (Winchester; York)
2 It was on Tower Hill, London.
3 It was established at Llantrisant, South Wales.
4 Britain's decimal currency was introduced on 15th February, 1971.
5 The metal ingots are melted in closed crucibles for about two hours and the molten metal is then run into moulds to form coinage-bars.
6 They are passed between rollers to ensure that they are of uniform size.
7 They are fed into annealing drums to soften the metal in preparation for the stamping process.
8 They are counted by an automatic machine.
9 Cupro-nickel is used in place of silver.
10 There would be two thousand 5p pieces.

Page 43 Using the right pronoun

1 I
2 me
3 I
4 me
5 me
6 I
7 me
8 I
9 I
10 me

Page 44 Alphabetical order

A

building
bus
fire-engine
helicopter
jet
motor-bike

B

1	shudder	2	passport	3	capsule
	signal		peculiar		chorus
	skier		physical		climate
	society		plumber		crusade
	student		portable		curfew

C

1	bladder	2	granite	3	sparrow
	bleak		grease		spectre
	blizzard		gristle		spiral
	blockade		ground		splint
	blunder		gruesome		sprawl

D

1	catalogue	2	problem	3	spray
	catch		proceed		spread
	catgut		produce		sprint
	catkin		profit		sprout
	cattle		promise		spruce
4	retail	5	patch	6	assault
	retire		patent		assets
	retort		patient		assist
	retreat		patriot		assorted
	return		pattern		assume

Page 45   Adjectives – formation

A

1	porous	5	spacious	8	perilous
2	famous	6	prosperous	9	villainous
3	envious	7	poisonous	10	gluttonous
4	vigorous				

B

1	humorous	5	furious	8	continuous
2	marvellous	6	mischievous	9	injurious
3	luxurious	7	riotous	10	miraculous
4	glorious				

Page 46 Joining sentences

A

1 The police arrested the youth who had robbed the bank.
2 Mrs. Baird gave Angela a bracelet which (that) was made of gold.
3 The door was opened by a young girl who looked very unhappy.
4 This is the house that Jack built.
5 Sitting near us was a woman whose hair had been dyed blue.

B

1 whose
2 who
3 which/that
4 whom
5 which/that

C
Own answers.

Page 47 Similes

A

1 deaf
2 bold
3 dead
4 clean
5 bee
6 cucumber
7 fiddle
8 button

B
Own answers.

C
Own answers.

Pages 48 and 49 Inside the vault

1 They are looking for the resting place of Thomas Kempe.
2 Bert will pretend that he is investigating the source of the rising damp.
3 Both effigies have been worn away by time in the centuries that have passed since they were first put there.
4 The statue's hands are as still as if they were frozen.
5 A hassock is a cushion especially made for kneeling on.
6 Bert knows the flagstone has been mortared in place because he did it.
7 James is the first of the three to look into the vault.
8 The small room is very dark because it is underground.
9 The boxes are coffins.
0 Thomas Kempe's box is by itself on the opposite side of the room to where all the other boxes are stacked.
1 31st October.
2 He died in the 17th century.
3 He was 62 years old. He would have been 63 on his next birthday.
4 He was an apothecary.
5 He was a sorcerer.
6 His true occupation could not be shown because the Church would not have allowed a sorcerer to be buried in the vault.
7 He believed in magic; and he hated priests.

Page 50   Joining sentences

A

Answers along the following lines.
1   The day was cold and windy for/as/because it was only the first day of February.
2   The children kept away from the dog because it was barking and trying to get over the gate.
3   The office had closed and the staff had departed although it was not yet five o'clock.
4   I had intended to go for a walk, but it started to snow and so I sat by the fire and fell fast asleep.
5   As Andrew had a bad leg and was unable to walk, he stayed indoors with Gillian, who read several stories to him.
6   We set off for the woods, but after a while, during a thunderstorm, we had to shelter in an old barn which was close at hand.

B

Own answers.

Page 51   Using the right verb

A

1	reveal	6	liberate	11	foreign language	16	promise
2	inflict	7	denounce	12	fortune	17	pests
3	evade	8	estimate	13	mob	18	catastrophe
4	impart	9	contract	14	request	19	statement
5	surmount	10	trespass	15	future	20	fine

B

1	inherit	3	disperse	5	impart	7	evaded
2	imposed	4	contracted	6	averted	8	estimated

Page 52   Idioms

A
1   to be under a cloud
2   to flog a dead horse
3   to be a dog in a manger
4   to draw the long bow
5   to bury the hatchet
6   to have an axe to grind
7   to take the bull by the horns
8   to be a wet blanket
9   to make a clean breast of it
10 to show the white feather
(And own answers.)

B
1   The detective was determined to take the bull by the horns.
2   Jamie told his uncle not to be a wet blanket.
3   The old rivals will soon bury the hatchet.
4   The prefect was under a cloud at school.
5   The old sailor is very found of drawing the long bow.

Page 53   Synonyms – similars

A

forbidden	4	room	7	try	9	height
smell	5	unbeatable	8	scatter	10	sudden
short	6	unwilling				

B

famous	4	hate	7	friendly	10	small
drunk	5	show	8	sad	11	sudden
understand	6	inside	9	pierce	12	smell

Page 54   A pony for Jody

He was caught by complete surprise when he saw the pony.
tense; disobedience.
He was choked with emotion.
Another word for **currying** is grooming/brushing/combing.
He warned him that he must feed the pony and clean his stall.
Jody was overcome by the sight of the pony and the thought that it might be for him.
Jody's fingers were bitten by the red pony.
Jody spoke of the pony with pride because he knew that the pony was going to be his.
They were relieved because Jody's words showed that he was pleased with the pony and this broke the tension of the situation.
Carl Tiflin wanted to be by himself because he was embarrassed.
He could not be ridden for some time because he was just a colt.
Billy Buck was going to help Jody break in the pony.

Page 55   Silent letters

A

ex**h**austed
cres**c**ent
psalm
moist**e**n
she**p**herd
pneumonia

B

1	pterodactyl	6	aghast
2	miscellaneous	7	heir
3	mortgage	8	dinghy
4	khaki	9	rhododendron
5	pseudonym	10	ptarmigan

Page 56   Sentence structure

A

1 Although she had been warned not to do so Julia persisted in talking.
2 Without thinking how she could pay for it she ordered the dress.
3 On the quay two sailors were having an argument.
4 Just as night was falling the convict was recaptured.
5 With a shriek of its whistle the express train rushed into the tunnel.
6 If you do not check that cough you will be seriously ill.
7 In the great hall of the castle a huge log fire blazed.
8 Long before daybreak the girl was up and about.

B

1 A Christmas Carol was written by Charles Dickens.
2 The Wanderers were beaten by the Rovers 2-0 last Saturday.
3 The valuable portrait was stolen by a gang of thieves.
4 The plans of the dining-hall were drawn by the County Architect.
5 The frail old gentleman was shaken by the heavy fall.
6 Spot was taken to the park by the twins.
7 That curtain was torn by our puppy.
8 The curtains for the lounge were chosen by the three girls.
9 Every single chocolate had been eaten by the one-eyed parrot.
10 The Ghost of Thomas Kempe was written by Penelope Lively.

Page 57   Alphabetical order

A

1	straight	2	handful	3	catacomb
	strand		handicap		catalogue
	strap		handle		catapult
	straw		handsome		cataract
	stray		handy		catastrophe

4	forth	5	partake	6	compare
	fortify		partial		compel
	fortnight		partly		compile
	fortress		partner		complain
	fortunate		party		compose

B

1	7	6	2	11	6	16	3
2	4	7	10	12	5	17	8
3	7	8	1	13	10	18	7
4	6	9	8	14	6	19	9
5	2	10	5	15	4	20	3

Page 58   Adjectives – formation

A

muscular	7	skilful	13	scientific
effective	8	beneficial	14	fiery
fraudulent	9	systematic	15	picturesque
athletic	10	creditable	16	influential
sympathetic	11	methodical	17	circular
energetic	12	gigantic	18	metallic

B

effective	5	scientific	9	nonsensical
skilful	6	circular	10	sympathetic
metallic	7	energetic	11	picturesque
athletic	8	beneficial	12	fraudulent

C

systematic	3	creditable	5	picturesque
methodical	4	customary		

Page 59   Capital letters

A

The River Thames is sometimes referred to as Old Father Thames.

Both German and Italian are taught at Grosvenor Grammar School.

Rudyard Kipling, who was born in India, wrote many fine books, the most famous being The Jungle Book.

Easter is a movable festival which may come in March or April, but Christmas is not.

The Bank of England is sometimes called The Old Lady of Threadneedle Street.

Linda's brother Colin is a patient at the Middlesex Hospital.

The White Tower in the Tower of London was built by Gundulf, Bishop of Rochester, about A.D. 1078.

From Monday to Friday the shop closes at 5.30; on Saturdays it closes at 1 o'clock.

B

Would you like to tour Europe and see its wonderful sights?

In the market there were ample supplies of apples, pears, oranges, bananas, peaches and grapes.

"James, did you give my message to the headmaster?" asked his mother.

"Yes, Mum, I gave it to him before lessons began," replied James.

Some members won't be present but it doesn't matter.

The ticket bore the date Thurs. 26th Sept. in bold type.

The bat we played with was Tom's but the ball was Duncan's.

"Oh dear," exclaimed Miss Taylor in alarm, "I have lost my purse!"

Page 60   Encounter with a dinosaur

1   The men were standing in the lighthouse tower.
2   The sound of the fog horn could be heard.
3   There was little visibility as the two men couldn't see far and they couldn't see plainly.
4   A ripple first told the men that there was something in the sea.
5   They saw the ripple far out at sea.
6   It rose a full forty feet.
7   The writer compares the monster's body to a little island of black coral and shells and crayfish.
8   It was ninety or a hundred feet long.
9   He suggested ten million years ago.
10 The monster was not continuously visible because its shape was sometimes blotted out by the fog coming and going about it.

Page 61   Homophones

A

1   veil
2   stationary
3   prophet
4   sow
5   muscle

B

1   herd; heard
2   key; quay
3   knight; night
4   stile; style
5   plaice; place

Page 62   Five familiar uses of the comma

1   "Your highness, your crown is crooked."
2   I have packed sweaters, socks and anoraks.
3   "Jake, can you hear me?"
4   "Can I help you, madam?"
5   "Yes, I want to buy a warm vest."
6   I've brushed the stairs, I've polished the furniture, I've cleaned the windows and now I'm going to have a rest.
7   "Good morning, Mrs. Brown."
8   David asked, "Are you awake?"
9   "I'm fast asleep," replied Tom quietly.
10 "I know very well," said David, "that you're wide awake."
11 "Anna and Matthew, it's time for bed."
12 Uncle Fred can speak German, French, Spanish, Italian and Russian.
13 As a matter of fact, you are right.
14 "Will you lock the door after you, please?"
15 "Hello, James."

Page 63   Rhymes

A

I		6	farms	11	flails
tower		7	see	12	floors
devour		8	be	13	doors
rye		9	arms	14	sails
flour		10	me	15	roars

B

decline		5	campaign	8	Antique
celebrate		6	interfere	9	rehearse
survey		7	receipt	10	picturesque
snare					

Pages 64 and 65   Prepositions

A

from		5	after	8	outside; around; at; near
along		6	around	9	on; across
before; near; by		7	through; over	10	off; from
against					

B

in; near; outside		5	between	8	at
into		6	among	9	beside; near
to		7	in	10	besides
with					

C

Own answers.

Page 66   Tarka fights Deadlock

Boulders; rocks, seaweed.
The animals were invading their territory.
They were watching the huntsman wading into the water.
People thought that Tarka had become exhausted and was now floating in the shallow water.
He shook his head because he could see no sign of the otter.
He prepared to sound his horn to call off the hunt.
Tarka's head appeared above the surface of the water.
Deadlock's struggle was in vain because Tarka's grip upon him was so tight.
Deadlock's hindlegs were above the surface of the water.
Tarka loosened his bite because he needed to breathe.
Fairway means "navigable channel'.
Flews means "hanging lips of a bloodhound".

Page 67   Containers

A

barrel

wallet

vase

dustbin

toolbox

crate

rucksack

cupboard

B

1 toolbox

2 crate

3 caddy

4 cupboard

5 wardrobe

6 holster

7 quiver

8 rucksack

9 manger

10 barrel

Page 68   Words with more than one meaning

A

1 litter

2 chest

3 charge

4 express

5 ground

6 spring

7 stern

8 plane

9 temple

10 coach

B

Own answers.

Page 69   Occupations

A

1 actress

2 physiotherapist

3 pilot

4 artist

5 surgeon

6 ballerina

7 photographer

8 teacher

B

1 taxidermist

2 interpreter

3 artist

4 beautician

5 pilot

6 engineers

7 solicitor

8 messenger

9 physiotherapist

10 surgeon

Page 70   Antonyms – opposites

A

contract	7	reward	13	reckless
defeat	8	minority	14	ascend
minimum	9	freedom	15	export
glut	10	superior	16	temporary
fine	11	exit	17	interior
decrease	12	opaque	18	voluntary

B

entrance	5	ancient	9	captivity
coarse	6	exterior	10	punishment
victory	7	attack	11	imports
compulsory	8	reckless	12	precise

Page 71   Hyphens

A

long-lost
grey-green
fifty-minute
old-fashioned
sixty-five

B

1 body-building
2 cupboard
3 merry-go-round
4 public house
5 lay-by

C

1 ridicu-lous
2 examina-tion

D

Own answers.

Page 72   Paragraph topics and sequencing

A

Tackling a project
My grandfather

B

1 c e d b a
2 e c b d a

C

Own answer.

D

Own answers.

Page 73   Agreement of subject and verb

A

has	3	wasn't	5	try	6	tries
have	4	weren't				

B

has	3	was	5	makes	7	are
have	4	were	6	make	8	is

Page 74   Metaphors

A

1   Clouds and boats.
    Both move at the same pace.
2   The ducks and us.
    Both hide by putting heads down (the ducks below water, people behind cover).
3   Reading and skimming.
    Both are quick and both just touch the surface.
4   Matthew and a wolf.
    Both eat quickly and hungrily.
5   My father and something exploding.
    Both happen unexpectedly and are noisy.

B

Own answers.

Page 75   Words which save work

A

1	recently	4	talkative	7	drought
2	surrendered	5	speechless	8	survivors
3	postponed	6	occasionally		

B

1	accidentally	4	fearlessly	6	apologized
2	immediately	5	librarian	7	revolved
3	author				

Page 76   Homophones

A

1	soar	4	site	7	horde	9	lessen
2	feint	5	berth	8	stake	10	route
3	bail	6	guilt				

Page 77   Noises of creatures

A

trumpeting	4	croaking	7	chattering	
barking	5	bleating	8	gobbling	
squealing	6	screeching; talking			

B

neigh	5	bulls	8	bay	
low	6	monkeys	9	sparrows	
growl	7	hyenas	10	turkeys	
apes					

C

bleating	4	chirping	6	trumpeted	
baying	5	screeching; talking	7	croaked	
bellowed					

Pages 78 and 79   Johann Gutenberg

Before printing was invented, books were handwritten.
a   There were very few books in existence.
b   Books were so valuable that they were locked away.
As a boy he spent hours watching goldsmiths stamping letters and figures on to coins. He also spent hours watching manuscripts being copied by hand. His invention brought both interests together.
To **pore** over a book is to study it very closely.
Laboriously means with great effort and a lot of work.
Each letter in Gutenberg's press was cut into an individual metal block.
Gutenberg contributed his technical knowledge and ideas. Fust provided the money to put them into practice.
300 copies were produced in 1456.
There were 1,282 pages in the Gutenberg Bible.
Johann Fust was greedy because he wasn't willing to share the profits. He wanted them all to himself. By demanding back from Gutenberg the money he had invested in the firm, he knew he was putting Gutenberg in an impossible position because he couldn't repay him. Fust was then able to claim all the working equipment in lieu and take over the firm.
Gutenberg earned nothing from his invention.
Possibly:
Para. 1   Earlier book production
Para. 2   Watching the goldsmiths
Para. 3   The invention of the printing press
Para. 4   Partnership with Fust
Para. 5   Personal ruin

Page 80   Sounds

A

1	bow	8	brook	15	clatter
2	bugle	9	whip	16	patter
3	bell	10	bagpipes	17	report
4	coins	11	swish	18	jangle; rattle
5	feet	12	rattle; clatter	19	clang
6	silk	13	pop	20	clap; peal
7	brakes	14	ping		

B

1	whirr	4	clang	7	skirl
2	peal	5	creak	8	throb
3	blast	6	wail		

Page 81   Doers of actions

A

1	challenger	6	critic
2	contributor	7	applicant
3	editor	8	operator
4	president	9	competitor
5	liar	10	survivor

B

1	burglar	6	representative
2	guardian	7	dictator
3	auctioneer	8	opponent
4	mutineer	9	successor
5	captor	10	correspondent

Pages 82 and 83   Three uses of the comma

A

Own answers (not necessarily wrong if they don't correspond to writers' own decisions).

B

The second sentence means that <u>all</u> the girls washed up.

C

1 My dog, a bulldog, terrifies everyone.
2 Prince Charles, the Queen's eldest son, is heir to the throne.
3 The prize, a trip to Alton Towers, was won by the headmaster.
4 I had my favourite meal, fish fingers and chips, since it was my birthday.
5 Her best friend, Zena Partridge, is leaving.

Page 84   A fight in a signal-tower

Marcus and Esca were by the parapet.
They dismounted in the courtyard below.
so far
Marcus thought that the tribesmen might be more useful to them alive than dead.
He kept it in his belt.
They were searching in the storehouse and guardroom.
Marcus described the tribesmen as fools because, by their shout, they had let Marcus and Esca know that they were coming up the stairway.
He had practised with the cestus.
The third tribesman, having seen his companions knocked down, had had some warning of what lay ahead of him.
He was unconscious.

Page 85   Double negatives

A

anything; nothing	7 anybody; nobody
anywhere; nowhere	8 any; no
anything; nothing	9 any; none
ever; never	10 anyone; no one
anything; nothing	11 anything; nothing
any; no	12 any; no

Page 86   More metaphors

A
Own answers along these lines.
Thinking of the **ebbing** of the tide, the gradual shrinking away of the sea from the shore, helps us to understand how gradually (but steadily) the light was going.
A rubber eraser can remove a pencilled drawing. It's a vivid comparison to make with the fog which covers the monster from sight for a moment just as effectively as if its picture had been rubbed out.
Rat plans to stay as close to Toad as if he were stuck to him with glue. It's vivid because it expresses Rat's determination to stay close and keep an eye on Toad (especially moving when it's a sense of duty that is making him stay).
This is a very vivid metaphor. A wave of sea water is powerful and crashes against any obstacle in its path. It makes the scent of the beanfield seem very intense and overpowering.
Ducks hide by putting their heads under the water. The tribesmen here are not hiding but lowering their heads to come through the doorway. The metaphor helps us to see the scene very clearly.

B
Own answers.

Page 87   Rhymes

A

1	bigger	5	thin	9	in	
2	figure	6	pin	10	kin	
3	head	7	skin	11	admire	
4	red	8	chin	12	attire	

B

1	work	4	course	7	nurse
	jerk		force		verse
	shirk		hoarse		worse
2	home	5	become	8	cheer
	foam		crumb		smear
	comb		glum		sphere
3	grows	6	stole	9	bought
	chose		shoal		caught
	froze		scroll		taut; taught

C

I have a garden of my own,
Shining with flowers of every hue;
I loved it dearly while alone,
But I shall love it more with you;
And there the golden bees shall come
In summer-time at break of morn,
And wake us with their busy hum,
Around the Silea's fragrant thorn.

Page 88   Direct speech revision

A

1 "How are you?" **a**sked Anne.
2 "I feel a bit sick," I said.
3 "Would you like to lie down**?**" she said kindly.
4 The shopkeeper smiled and murmured**,** "What can I do for you, madam?"
5 "Just as we turned off the main road," said Elaine**,** "a huge coach came roaring towards us!"

B

See relevant passage on Page 6.

Page 89   Idioms

through the nose
feathering one's nest
to play second fiddle
to smell a rat
blowing his own trumpet

6   at loggerheads
7   a mountain out of a molehill
8   sent him to Coventry
9   French leave
10   the cold shoulder

Page 90   Long John Silver

The nickname was Barbecue.
He carried it by a lanyard round his neck.
It enabled him to have both hands as free as possible.
He wedged the foot of the crutch against a bulkhead to steady himself.
He had a line or two rigged up to help him across the widest spaces.
The coxswain told of the time when John, unarmed, had grappled four men and knocked their heads together.
The crew respected John for his learning, bravery and strength.
The parrot's name was Captain Flint.
Pirate is another word for buccaneer.
He would throw his handkerchief over the cage.